STARK

ABITUR-WISSEN

Landeskunde USA

Rainer Jacob

© 2018 Stark Verlag GmbH
www.stark-verlag.de
1. Auflage 2001

Inhalt

Vorwort

Autor: Rainer Jacob

Vorwort

Liebe Schülerinnen, liebe Schüler,

in den Englisch-Lehrplänen werden neben sprachlichen Fertigkeiten auch landeskundliche bzw. soziokulturelle Kenntnisse und interkulturelle Kompetenz gefordert. Geographisches, historisches, politisches und kulturelles Wissen ist unabdingbar zum Verständnis aktueller Entwicklungen in den wichtigsten englischsprachigen Ländern. Dieser Band hilft Ihnen bei der **Vorbereitung auf Ihre Klausuren und das Abitur**, indem er das relevante Wissen über die Vereinigten Staaten übersichtlich und prägnant vorstellt.

Land und Leute in den USA kann man erst begreifen, wenn man die **Wurzeln der amerikanischen Nation** kennt, und z. B. die politischen Gegebenheiten, die Aufgabenteilung zwischen den Staaten und der Bundesregierung, die Rolle des Supreme Court und die Rolle der Medien.

Dieses Buch ist in **verständlichem Englisch** verfasst, um Sie an das Niveau der mündlichen und schriftlichen Prüfungen zu gewöhnen. Jedes Kapitel ist in sich abgeschlossen und **sinnvoll untergliedert**, sodass Sie sich gezielt über abiturrelevante Aspekte der einzelnen Themenbereiche informieren können. **Zahlreiche Bilder** veranschaulichen die im Text erläuterten Fakten, **Schaubilder** stellen wichtige Zusammenhänge dar.

Ich wünsche Ihnen viel Erfolg bei Ihrer Vorbereitung und hoffe, dass Sie auch einige bisher unbekannte Seiten des „Landes der unbegrenzten Möglichkeiten" für sich entdecken.

Rainer Jacob

The Constitution of the United States

The constitution of a democratic country defines its political institutions and contains the basic laws upon which all other laws are founded. This description of the political system and the rights and duties of the citizens are usually assembled in a single document such as the German "**Grundgesetz**". Britain is an exception among modern democracies – it has no written constitution. This is so because England was the first country in which the principles of democracy and parliamentary government developed over the course of several hundred years. This process began in the 13th century when the English King John was forced to sign **Magna Carta**, which limited the powers of the Crown. With the passing of the Bill of Rights in 1689, which extended the powers of Parliament, the foundations of democratic institutions were finally laid. The British model of democracy had evolved and was a model for other countries. The advantage for the new democracies was that they could profit from the experiences gained in Britain, and eventually work out an even fairer and more up-to-date system. This was the case in the United States where the **Founding Fathers** of the nation used the British system as their blueprint and improved it by including political theories of British and French philosophers of the Age of Enlightenment. Among these modern ideas which had never been worked out in practice in the Old World were: the separation of church and state, the sovereignty of the people, government by the people and effective checks and balances in government. Thus the United States became the first country in which these progressive concepts were transferred into political reality. However, this step forward did not come easily – self-determination was only achieved after a long struggle of the colonists in the New World against British rule.

Historical Background

The battle for dominance on the American Continent between the two major powers England and France was decided in the **Seven Years' War (1756–1763)**, the result being that France lost her influence and Britain gained sole control of North America. Now that the French competition was eliminated, a sensible and intelligent monarch was needed to handle the administration of the British colonies in North America. In 1760, **George III** became King of

England, and, unfortunately, the incapability of the new sovereign soon became evident. Instead of granting the prospering colonies more freedom, the king and his advisors tried to exert more control and reduce self-government.

The interests of the colonists and those of the mother country soon collided. The first point of contention was the westward expansion of the colonies. More land for settlement was needed because the population was increasing fast. The British government, however, did not want to fulfil these demands because it feared that if settlers moved further west the Indian wars would erupt again. Therefore a **Royal Proclamation** was issued in 1763 prohibiting land conquest in the western territory between the Alleghenies, Florida, the Mississippi River and Quebec. This measure was totally ineffective, yet it contributed to a growing dissatisfaction on the side of the colonists with their mother country. The colonists felt neglected and exploited. They had the feeling that Britain was only interested in taking advantage of the colonies in order to increase her own economic position and prosperity. This impression was soon confirmed by the financial policy which the British adopted in the colonies.

A number of new laws were passed in London as the king needed more and more money to support the growing empire. The **Sugar Act** of 1764 put duties on molasses, wines, silks, coffee and a number of other luxury items and forbade the importation of foreign rum. Merchants in New England protested against the new tax because, they argued, the payments would ruin their business. The **Stamp Act** of 1765 increased taxes on newspapers and printed matter in the colonies. The tax laws caused serious tensions between the colonials and the British Parliament and culminated in the slogan **"no taxation without representation"**. The colonists were no longer willing to pay taxes to their mother country without being properly represented in the House of Commons at Westminster, where the laws were passed. The colonists did not question the sovereignty of the king but they denied parliament the right to pass laws without them being consulted first. The response of the British parliament to this demand was the passage of the **Declaratory Act** (1766). It affirmed the authority of the British parliament to make laws binding on the colonies – an insult for the colonists and at the same time an illustration of how insensitive the parliamentarians in London were towards the maturing 13 colonies across the Atlantic.

The American Revolution

In this atmosphere of growing tension two events happened in Boston which eventually sparked off the American Revolution. In 1770, British troops occupying Boston to enforce the new British taxes fired into a mob of about 60 Bostonians outside the Old State House. Five demonstrators were killed in the incident which became known as the **Boston Massacre**. Three years later, on December 16, 1773, a large crowd of colonists gathered at the Old South Meeting House to protest against the monopoly of the East India Company and a tax on tea. Disguised as Mohawk Indians, about 60 American patriots threw 342 chests of tea from ships belonging to the East India Company into Boston Harbour. Angered by the **Boston Tea Party**, the British closed the port of Boston to trade until its citizens compensated the East India Company for the destroyed tea, and parliament in Westminster passed a series of new laws, the **Coercive Acts**, to punish the colonists. In order to repeal these suppressive regulations, which the colonists called **Intolerable Acts**, representatives of twelve colonies (with the exception of Georgia) met in the **First Continental Congress** in Philadelphia. When on April 19, 1775, British troops tried to seize the arms of colonists at Lexington, Massachusetts, the first shot was fired. The **War of Independence**, which was to last till 1783, had begun.

A clash between colonists and a squad of British troops (left) became known as the Boston Massacre – an incident which eventually led to the Boston Tea Party in 1773 (above) and the outbreak of the American War of Independence.

George Washington

On May 10, 1775, the **Second Continental Congress** assembled in Philadelphia and made George Washington (1732–1799) commander of the American forces. The command was an honour, but Washington knew very well that it was a formidable task, too. He had to organize an army out of about 16,000 men, who were inexperienced in fighting and lacked military discipline. Baron von Steuben, a Prussian officer, joined the American forces and helped to drill and organize the troops. Out of necessity, Washington applied a new fighting technique. His men did not confront the enemy in formation, but attacked in small groups, spreading themselves all over the place. On July 4, 1776, the colonies declared their independence from Britain. In the winter of the same year Washington crossed the Delaware, captured the city of Trenton and took about one thousand prisoners. The British soldiers – called Redcoats because of their uniform – fought back, but had great problems in trying to transport men and weapons because Washington's army frequently cut their supply lines. The tables turned when in May 1778, the French, Britain's old enemy from the Seven Years' War, came to the aid of the colonists. The British commander Lord Cornwallis surrendered his entire army at Yorktown on October 19, 1781, and two years later, in 1783, the final peace treaty, the **Treaty of Paris**, was signed. George Washington, the hero of the new nation, who had led the United States to victory over Britain, was **elected president** in 1789 and re-elected in 1792. Both times he received every vote cast by the electors.

The Declaration of Independence

The **Declaration of Independence** was written in 1776, and adopted by the American Congress in Philadelphia on 4 July of the same year. Since then the **4th of July** has been celebrated as **Independence Day** in the United States. When the Declaration was signed, a bell was rung, the Liberty Bell, which has become one of the most famous symbols of American independence. It was cast in England, in 1752, originally to commemorate Pennsylvania's Charter of Privileges. When the bell reached America, it was cracked and had to be re-cast. Until 1835, when it cracked again, it was rung every 4th of July. In 1976, to mark the Bicentenary of the Declaration of Independence, Queen Elizabeth presented a new bell to the people of the USA. Engraved on this new bell, which was from the same foundry as the Liberty Bell, are the words "Let Freedom Ring". Taken from a hymn, these words were used on August 28, 1963, by Martin Luther King in his speech "I have a dream".

Historical Background

In 1776 – the 13 colonies were still at war with Britain – many people belived-ed that a solution to the problems between the colonists and the mother country would eventually be found. Only a minority believed in complete independence. But as anger towards the British grew, Congress decided that all links with the mother country should be cut. Five of the members of Congress were asked to write a formal Declaration of Independence. Among them was **Thomas Jefferson** (1743–1826), a representative of the state of Virginia, who later became the nation's third president (1801–1809). He wrote the first draft of the original document, working at his desk in the home of a young German bricklayer, Jacob Graff. Jefferson finished his work in two weeks, Benjamin Franklin and John Adams later made some minor changes.

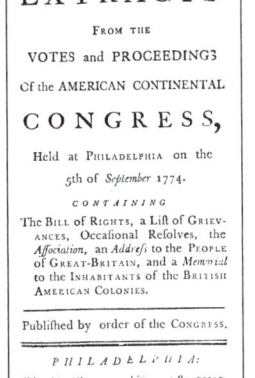

EXTRACTS

FROM THE

VOTES and PROCEEDINGS

Of the AMERICAN CONTINENTAL

CONGRESS,

Held at PHILADELPHIA on the
5th of *September* 1774.

CONTAINING

The BILL of RIGHTS, a Lift of GRIEV-
ANCES, Occafional Refolves, the
Affociation, an *Addrefs* to the PEOPLE
of GREAT-BRITAIN, and a *Memorial*
to the INHABITANTS of the BRITISH
AMERICAN COLONIES.

Publifhed by order of the CONGRESS.

PHILADELPHIA:
Printed by WILLIAM and THOMAS BRADFORD,
October 27th, M,DCC,LXXIV.

From 1774 to 1789 delegates of the North American colonies convened at several meetings. The first of these congresses was held in Philadelphia in 1774. Among the representatives assembled were George Washington (picture on the left) and John Adams. In 1775, Benjamin Franklin and Thomas Jefferson (picture on the right) joined the delegates.

Equality and Human Rights

The Declaration of Independence begins with an indirect attack on the British king for his tyrannical rule. The colonists derive their right to resistance from the monarch's unfair administration. They hold George III responsible for the revolution and justify their rebellion. In the second sentence Thomas Jefferson and his co-authors express two revolutionary concepts, which have made the Declaration of Independence so influential, the ideas of **equality and natural rights**. Jefferson proclaims that "all men are created equal", which means that birth and position are irrelevant. It is not important whether somebody is born into a royal family or into a poor peasant's household. What is more, not only are all people equal, each individual also enjoys certain rights, which nobody can take away. These are rights which every human being has. They include the right of **life, liberty** and the **pursuit of happiness**. The right of liberty means that nobody can be imprisoned or sentenced to death without a fair trial. Everybody has the right to choose their own way of life, to decide where they want to live, what they are going to do with their life – to be happy. This idea of the "pursuit of happiness" is the basis of the individualism of the American people, their firm belief in everybody's right – and choice – to decide for themselves where their happiness lies.

Thomas Jefferson was not the author of this theory. The concept of natural rights was worked out in the 17th and 18th centuries when French, German and English philosophers (René Descartes, Gottfried Leibniz, Francis Bacon) questioned political absolutism, the unlimited, centralized authority in the hands of a monarch. The most notorious example being the French King Louis XIV, who said, "L'état, c'est moi" ("I am the state"). Thomas Jefferson used the writings of the most important natural-law theorist of the 18th century, the English philosopher **John Locke** (1632–1704), to phrase the Declaration of Independence. The great achievement of the American colonists lies in the fact that they, for the first time in modern history, used the most advanced philosophical theories to establish a new nation.

The Sovereignty of the People and the Role of Government

The Declaration of Independence clearly states the relation between a government and the people. All power lies with the people ("Alle Macht geht vom Volk aus."), and the only function of any government is to make sure that the people can exercise their natural rights. This means the government must provide the framework within which each individual can lead their own life according to their personal wishes and aspirations. If a government fails in this role, if it abuses its power, the people have the right to overthrow the government. Here again, the main source which Jefferson used were the writings of John Locke. In his **Treatises of Government** (1690) Locke had written a justification of the Glorious Revolution in England and denied the king the divine right to govern. He expanded the "contract theory" of government, the main argument of which was that all just governments were founded on consent and their only task was to protect people in their natural rights to life, liberty, and property.

Jefferson's words about the role of a government are still very much alive in American politics. In 1981, in his first inaugural address, President Ronald

Reagan of the Republican Party stressed the fact that Americans had always believed in government "of the people, by the people and for the people". Consequently, men do not owe their allegiance to a government or its leaders. For Jefferson, dissent was not only a right but also a necessity. "I hold that a little rebellion now and then is a good thing", he said.

Theory and Reality
"We hold these truths to be self-evident, that all men are created equal, that they are endowed by their Creator with certain unalienable Rights, that among these are Life, Liberty and the pursuit of Happiness." – The notion expressed by the Founding Fathers that America is the country which offers freedom and equal chances is one of the basic convictions upon which America's pride is founded. It is an ideal which Americans have cherished until today – although there has always been a difference between theory and reality. Even in the days when the Declaration of Independence was signed this ideal state of equality did not exist because, for example, black people, and women, were not included. All of the signatories were white males of European descent, most of them wealthy property holders who owned black slaves – as did Thomas Jefferson. Nevertheless, in 1963, Martin Luther King referred to the Declaration of Independence when he told the masses about his dream of a united and free America.

Today equality still seems a long way off in the United States for the disadvantaged, the working poor and other social groups which are confronted with discrimination on the grounds of their race, sex or age. For them the American Dream is still a dream, something which they find hard or even impossible to fulfil. It is mostly members of minority groups, such as African Americans, Native Americans, or Hispanics who to a great degree do not participate in the prosperity of the country. As former president Barack Obama once told the nation, "Structural inequalities – from disparities in education and health care to the vicious cycle of poverty – still pose enormous hurdles for black communities across America."

Today, it is also white, less-educated citizens, who feel increasingly left out and behind. In the "Rust Belt" states of the North East, for example, many workers lost their jobs (mostly in coal mining, steel production and motor manufacturing) due to globalisation and automation. In the 2016 US presidential election the Republican candidate Donald Trump gained a high share of votes from disillusioned voters with his pledge that "the forgotten men and women of our country will be forgotten no longer".

The Importance of the Declaration of Independence

Apart from its immediate purpose to provide a legitimation of the American Revolution the Declaration is a remarkable document because it proclaimed the principles of human rights and defined the **role of government**. Because of the clarity and the determination with which these new ideas were expressed the document has been regarded as the "first declaration of human rights" and it has become the "cornerstone of modern democracies". In 1789, during the French Revolution, the National Assembly of France adopted the **Declaration of the Rights of Man and of the Citizen**, which echoes the principles expressed in Jefferson's document. In the late 18th and the 19th century the concept of human rights as expressed in the Declaration of Independence was further advanced. In the 19th century, various peoples of Europe and of Latin America worked out their political systems by incorporating the ideas formulated by Thomas Jefferson. Germany's *Grundgesetz* (1949), which was elaborated after the end of World War II when the horrors of the "Third Reich" were still very much alive, owes a great deal to the values of the Declaration of Independence.

The Declaration of Independence was written by Thomas Jefferson in June 1776. Later changes were added by John Adams and Benjamin Franklin.

Today there is general agreement in Western countries that all human beings are entitled to some basic rights and that the observance of human rights is the most important feature of a democratic state. In the charter establishing the United Nations, all members were pledged to achieve "universal respect for, and observance of, human rights." The UN has continued to affirm its commitment to human rights, particularly in such documents as the **Universal Declaration of Hu-**

man Rights (1948). Today the original document of the Declaration of Independence is on view at the National Archives Building in Washington, D.C.

The Constitution

Historical Background

The **War of Independence** ended in 1783 with the victory of the colonists over their former mother country Britain. The Americans now faced the long and exhausting task of building their own independent nation. In 1777, while still at war with the British, the Americans had adopted their first constitution, the **Articles of Confederation**, which were ratified in 1781. This first constitution replaced an informal union of the thirteen states with a central, but very weak, government. It soon became evident that the system did not work, because it left too much sovereignty to the states. On the economic side for example, the central government had no authority to control trade and remove commercial barriers between the states so that in the end all states suffered financially. In international politics America's voice was not listened to because of the lack of unity among the states. At home, **Shays' Rebellion**, an armed outbreak by debtor farmers in western Massachusetts in 1786/87, and unrest on the Western frontier increased fears that the union would not survive. In 1787, Alexander Hamilton (representative of New York) and George Washington (representative of Virginia) managed to persuade the 13 states to send representatives to meet in Philadelphia to discuss the problems and decide on a new form of government. The legislatures sent their best men, among them James Madison from Virginia and Benjamin Franklin from Pennsylvania. Rhode Island was not represented and the only important men missing were Thomas Jefferson and John Adams, who held diplomatic posts, representing the United States abroad. George Washington was elected president of the meeting which became known as the **Constitutional Convention** and lasted till 17 September. The politicians assembled in a building which was then the State House of the Province of Pennsylvania and is today known as Independence Hall, the same building in which the Declaration of Independence had been adopted nine years earlier.

The Framing of the Constitution

The enormous challenge for the representatives assembled in Philadelphia was to create a constitution which would hold the large and diverse nation together and, at the same time, protect the rights of the people. There were two opposing views as to how the union could be governed efficiently and also how the government could be controlled. One group, the **Federalists**, advocated the establishment of a powerful government, whereas the other party, the **anti-Federalists**, believed in leaving most power and responsibilities in the hands of the individual states. They looked upon a strong central agency with suspicion. As both sides presented good arguments for their convictions, it was clear that only a compromise could bridge the differences of opinion. James Madison from Virginia became the principal architect of the Constitution. Convinced that the prosperity of the country depended on a strong union he favoured a strong central government and presented his plan according to which the government was to consist of three branches – executive, judiciary, and legislative. This **Virginia Plan** did not appeal to the anti-Federalists because they felt too much power was being conferred to the central government. In order to dispel the doubts of the anti-Federalists a new solution had to be found. The problem was solved by Connecticut delegates Sherman and Ellsworth, who presented their **Great Compromise** in which Madison's suggestions were supplemented with the creation of a legislature composed of two houses: the Senate and the House of Representatives. The plan provided for equal voting in the Senate and proportional representation in the House of Representatives. This explains why Congress today comprises 100 members in the Senate – two from each state, irrespective of size and population – and of a varying number of members according to state populations in the House of Representatives. After prolonged debates and discussions the new plan was accepted and the Constitution was eventually drafted in September 1787. It was agreed that the supreme law of the land should be binding on all states and therefore had to be ratified by 9 of the 13 states before it could become law. In some states, particularly in Virginia and New York, there was still strong opposition led by the most prominent anti-Federalist Patrick Henry. It was mainly because of the forceful rhetoric of James Madison and Alexander Hamilton that the wavering states could in the end be convinced to agree to the compromise. The Constitution was ratified in 1788 and put into effect in 1789.

Preamble and Seven Articles

The representatives at the convention did not try to cover every possible eventuality, they preferred the Constitution of the United States to be short. It is composed of a Preamble, seven articles, and (in the meantime) twenty-seven amendments. An amendment is a change of or addition to the Constitution. The preamble states the reasons for adopting a constitution. Article I deals with the powers of Congress, the composition of the House and Senate and election to them, and restrictions upon the powers of the states. Article II covers the presidency, including election and powers, while Article III outlines the powers and responsibilities of the judiciary. Article IV describes relations between states and the admission of new states. In Article V the authors laid down how amendments to the Constitution should be made because they realised that with the development of the new republic changes might be required. An amendment may be made by a two-thirds vote of both houses of Congress and ratification by three-fourths of the states. Article VI states the authority of the Constitution; and Article VII says that nine states will have to ratify the Constitution before it becomes effective.

The Bill of Rights

When the Constitution was written, several states claimed it did not clearly guarantee the rights and freedoms that had been fought for in the American Revolution. In their eyes the Constitution merely provided rules for the machinery of government. Consequently, they refused to sign the document unless a number of amendments to the Constitution were added to provide more protection for individuals. These **first ten amendments** became known as the **Bill of Rights**, and they are a summary of the most important rights held by all US citizens. Canada has a similar summary, called the Charter of Rights and Freedoms. The Bill of Rights, which was passed by Congress in 1789 and became law in 1791, limits the authority of the government and guarantees the fundamental rights of all citizens. It is important to note that there is a difference between "human rights" and "civil rights". Every human being enjoys human rights, which belief was clearly expressed in the Declaration of Independence. However, not all people living in a country have civil rights, such as the right to vote, the freedom of speech, of press and of religion – the reason being that they are inhabitants of a country but not citizens, perhaps they are foreigners or below the age of majority, or serving sentences in prison. The Bill of Rights has been called **"the real bulwark"** of American personal liberties. All over the world, from Europe to South Africa, countries have worked out their democratic systems using the Bill of Rights as the example to follow. The respect for civil rights – as well as human rights – has become a crucial test for any government's legitimacy. However, it is not only the government but also the people who should contribute to the good of society as John F. Kennedy told the nation in 1961: "And so, my fellow Americans: ask not what your country can do for you – ask what you can do for your country."

The **First Amendment** of the Constitution of the United States guarantees freedom of religion, speech, press, and assembly. The **Second** secures the right to bear arms: "A well-regulated militia being necessary to the security of a free state, the right of the people to keep and bear arms shall not be infringed." This amendment is used by American gun owners organised in the National Rifle Association to prevent stricter gun control laws; they call the Second Amendment their "Second Amendment birthright". The **Third** Amendment protects citizens against soldiers being quartered in private homes. The **Fourth** Amendment is the American equivalent to the British motto "Every man's house is his castle" because it protects people and their houses against unlawful entry, unreasonable search and seizure. The US Supreme Court has ruled since 1961 that evidence obtained by police by breaking into a suspect's home cannot be used in court. If the police do not have a warrant, for example, they are not allowed to enter a private house to look for evidence.

The **Fifth** Amendment concerns a person's right to remain silent in a court trial in order not to incriminate himself or herself. This provision of the Bill of Rights was often referred to in the highly publicised O. J. Simpson trial, and it plays a major role in the popular novels of John Grisham. When cross-examined in court a defendant may "take the Fifth", which means he refuses to answer a question because his reply might be used against him. The Supreme Court ruled in 1966 that suspects have to be informed about their right not to say anything and to have a lawyer present if they wish.

Further Amendments
Since 1791, further amendments have been added, among them the so-called **Civil War Amendments** (Thirteen, 1865; Fourteen, 1868; Fifteen, 1870) which outlawed slavery, declared all people born or naturalised in the United States to be citizens, and that the right to vote could not be denied because of colour. The **Fourteenth** Amendment of 1868 served as the legal basis in the fight for racial equality by the protestors of the Civil Rights Movement. The **Nineteenth** Amendment (1920) gave women the right to vote, the **Twenty-Third** Amendment (1961) extended the right to vote in presidential elections to residents of Washington in the District of Columbia. The voting age was lowered to 18 by the **Twenty-Sixth** Amendment (1971). The Founding Fathers put high obstacles in the path of passing new amendments; the latest number **Twenty-Seven** is about Congressional pay increases and was ratified in 1992.

Thousands of proposals have been made to amend the Constitution, but only 33 obtained the necessary two-thirds vote in Congress. Of those 33, only 27 amendments (including the Bill of Rights) have been ratified. In the year 2000, for example, great parts of the American public discussed the question whether the US flag needed constitutional protection. Patriotic Americans deplored the desecration of the flag often printed on trivial articles such as T-shirts, jeans, and coffee mugs, and that it was shown freely in advertisements. They maintained that this disrespectful use was an insult to America's veterans and to the nation and called for an amendment to the Constitution to protect the flag. A first step was taken in the House of Representatives where a bill was passed to enable Congress to enact legislation. However, after heated discussions, the US Senate narrowly defeated the proposed constitutional amendment, four short of the two-thirds majority needed. Many senators

President Abraham Lincoln's (1861–65) Emancipation Proclamation of 1863 freed the slaves. In 1865, the abolition of slavery became part of the constitution as the Thirteenth Amendment.

argued that the flag, while a precious symbol, was above the need for such protection. In 2006, the last attempt to add a Flag Desecration Amendment failed.

The System of Government

Creating a Federal Government

In 1787, fifty-five delegates of the newly-founded "United States of America" met in Philadelphia to amend the "Articles of Confederation", a compact which the 13 colonies had adopted in 1781. The bitter years of the **War of Independence** with their former mother country England had taught the colonists that the loose association which they had agreed upon in the "Articles" was too weak to manage the problems of the fledgling nation. Problems abroad and at home continued to grow. There was no uniform stable currency in the 13 states, each printed its own money. Several states quarrelled over state boundaries. In Massachusetts, a former Revolutionary War army captain, Daniel Shaw, led a rebellion of impoverished farmers. In short, it was a time of turmoil and chaos. Calls for a strong central government were supported by war hero George Washington, who warned: "There are combustibles in every state which a spark might set fire to." The main task of the Constitutional Convention, therefore, was to improve the **Articles of Confederation**. Very soon, however, this aim was abandoned and the delegates opted for a more comprehensive and radical solution. They worked out a completely new political system for the new-born nation instead, the basics of which they laid down in the **United States Constitution**.

The Separation of Power

The framers of the Constitution achieved two aims: they created a federal government with far-reaching authority and secured the protection of the rights of individual people at the same time. The foundation of the system is the firm conviction that final authority is vested in the people – a belief which had already been expressed in the **Declaration of Independence**. The people do not exercise their authority directly, they delegate it to officials who carry out the day-to-day business of governing the nation. To avoid an excessive concentration of authority, as existed then in the monarchies in Europe, power was separated into three branches – the executive branch, the legislative branch and the judiciary branch. All three branches were equally important and each branch controlled the others. The system was effective enough to govern four million people in 13 different colonies along the Atlantic coast at the end of the eighteenth century. Today the same system, with only 27 amendments, serves the needs of more than 320 million people in 50 states. This proves the strength and soundness of the framework conceived in Philadelphia in 1787 and makes the American Constitution the world's oldest written constitution in force. Moreover, countries all over the world have used it as the model to organise their democracies.

The Executive Branch

The Office of President

The delegates at the Constitutional Convention unanimously elected George Washington the first president, John Adams was voted vice-president. Both were sworn into office on April 30, 1789, in New York, which Congress had fixed as the seat of the new government. In 1800, the capital of the new republic was moved to Washington in the District of Columbia (D.C.). A grey sandstone building which was painted white, aptly named **White House**, has since been both residence and office of the US president. The Constitution requires the president to be a native-born American citizen of at least 35 years of age who must have lived in the United States for at

The White House, on Pennsylvania Avenue, Washington, D.C., is the official residence of the US president.

least 14 years. He is elected by the people through the Electoral College to a four-year term and can be re-elected once.

The president's chief duty is to protect the Constitution and enforce the laws made by Congress, which means he has to sign the bills before they can become law. A look at the president's further functions makes his powerful position obvious. He is **Head of the Executive** and also **Head of State**, he is the **commander-in-chief** of the country's armed forces and in times of emergency can give executive orders that do not have to be passed by Congress.

He has overall responsibility for formulating and executing the foreign policy of the United States and participates in summit conferences where chiefs of state meet for direct consultation. Almost all American presidents in the 20th and 21st century have been actively involved in world politics. President Woodrow Wilson headed the American delegation to the Paris conference at the end of World War I; President Franklin D. Roosevelt conferred with the Allied leaders at sea, in Africa and in Asia during World War II. President Clinton played an important role as conciliator between Palestinians and Israelis in the Middle East conflict.

The president also appoints **Supreme Court** judges and ambassadors, and chooses the heads of all executive departments and agencies. He also has the pardoning power to shorten prison terms or reduce fines of people who have been convicted of breaking the law. Because of the vast range of responsibilities which a president holds some political analysts have spoken of the "imperial presidency", meaning the position is so powerful that it resembles that of a monarch of old times, especially when the office is in the hands of a strong personality. However, in the Constitution the Founding Fathers laid down one measure which can be used to remove the president from office if he abuses his authority and fails in his duties.

Removing a President: Impeachment

The public demands that the incumbent in the White House observes a higher moral standard than ordinary people. John Steinbeck characterised the very special relationship of the American people to their president like this: "We have established a tough but unwritten code of behaviour for him, and the slightest error causes a lot of exaggerated accusations. We subject him and his family to constant examination and accuse them for things that we ourselves do every day." In 1998, a storm broke loose over President Clinton's personal conduct. His opponents accused him of obstructing justice to cover up an affair he was supposed to have had with Monica Lewinsky, a young White House trainee, and asked him to resign. Clinton refused and the opposition tried to remove the president from office on **impeachment** – a drastic measure provided for in Article II, Section 4 of the Constitution.

The impeachment process is a trial which goes through eight stages. Stage 1 is the resolution in the House of Representatives, the final stage is the Senate vote, when the Senators vote on each article of impeachment. If a two-thirds majority supports impeachment, the president is removed from office. Since 1789 only nineteen federal officials, fifteen judges and two presidents have been impeached. Seven were convicted by the Senate. Most impeachment resolutions that have been filed against presidents have died in the initial stages (in the **House Judiciary Committee**), only few went further. In 1843 President John Tyler was charged of corruption and misconduct. Tyler followed the impeachment process until stage 3, when the House rejected the charges. In 1868, the charge against President Andrew Johnson was serious misconduct. He followed the impeachment process until final stage 8, the

Senate vote, where he was acquitted by a margin of one vote. Johnson completed his term. In 1974, following the **Watergate Scandal**, the charge against President Richard Nixon was obstruction and abuse of power. Nixon followed the impeachment process up to stage 6, but resigned before the final vote was taken. The impeachment against President Bill Clinton began in September 1998. The **independent counsel**, Kenneth W. Starr, sent a report to the House saying he had found "substantial and credible information" constituting grounds for impeachment of President Clinton. The charges were perjury and obstruction of justice. Clinton went through the whole trial and, on February 12, 1999, was acquitted by the Senate. All these months the executive had been paralysed, because not only people in America but all over the whole world were

Protest against the Clinton impeachment

waiting for the final outcome of the proceedings. What it showed in the end was that not even the most powerful person in the world, the US president, is above the law. If the president really fails in his duties and in his conduct, he can be removed from office.

The Departments and Agencies

Fourteen **departments and a number of executive agencies**, such as the National Security Council, the Office of Management and Budget, the Council of Economic Advisers, assist the president in the daily administration of the affairs of the country. The heads of the departments, chosen by the president and approved by the Senate, form a council of advisers generally known as the **President's Cabinet**. Departments are, for example, the Department of State, which advises the president on foreign policy, the Department of Defense, which has its headquarter in the Pentagon, the "world's largest office building", the Department of Agriculture, which supervises agricultural production, or the Department of Education.

A special section of the Department of Justice has gained more importance today, it is the Drug Enforcement Administration (DEA). It is concerned with the fight against mafia-like organisations involved in the growing, manufacture, or distribution of drugs in the US and on international markets.

In order to keep the government and the economy working smoothly there are a number of so-called **independent agencies** which are not part of the executive departments. These agencies include the Central Intelligence Agency (CIA), which collects and evaluates intelligence information and makes recommendations to the National Security Council. The Environmental Protection Agency (EPA), founded in 1970, whose primary function is to control pollution in the air and water, and to deal with the problems of solid waste, pesticides, radiation and toxic substances. The National Aeronautics and Space Administration (NASA), established in 1958 to run the US space programme, placed the first American satellites and astronauts in orbit, and launched the Apollo spacecraft that landed men on the moon in 1969.

All these departments and agencies form the executive branch of the federal government – a large organisation employing several million people. The president is the head of the civilian government work force, but he appoints only about 3,000 of them. The vast majority are civil servants who work independently of the government of the day.

Presidential against Parliamentary Government

Time and again political scientists have argued for the transformation of the American system of presidential government into one resembling a parliamentary system as it is practised in Britain. The main differences between the two systems concern the relationship between the executive and the legislature. In Britain, the executive consists of several members: the prime minister, the leader of the majority party, and his cabinet, who are chosen by, chosen from and remain members of the House of Commons. In the USA, there is a single executive, the president, who is elected by the voters for a fixed term and his office is separate from the legislature. In Britain, members of the executive are responsible to and can be removed by parliament whereas in the United States it is very difficult to remove the president from office. Another feature is that in Britain – and in Germany – the offices of Head of State and Head of the Executive are separate. The queen or president stay above party politics, they try to speak for and represent all the people. In the US, both offices are combined in the president who may claim to be acting for all the people when in fact he is acting as party leader. The advantage of the system of parliamentary government is that the executive can carry out its programmes rapidly, because it usually has a majority in parliament. The president's intentions can be delayed by Congress. The presidential system, on the other hand, provides stable government, cabinet overthrows and unforeseen elections are unknown, which make effective government more likely.

The Legislative Branch

Congress, the legislature of the United States of America, is composed of two chambers, the **Senate** and the **House of Representatives**. The creation of this system is the result of the discussions at the Constitutional Convention in Philadelphia in 1787. The representatives of the larger states argued in favour of proportional representation in the nation's legislature – each state should have voting power according to its population. The smaller states, fearing domination by the larger ones, insisted on equal representation for all states. The issue was settled by the "Great Compromise", giving every state equal representation in one house of Congress, and proportional representation in the other. This is why today the Senate consists of 100 senators, two from each state. Wyoming, the least populous of the American states, has as many senators as California, the state with the most inhabitants. Senators rank very high socially, behind the president and vice-president. They must be at least 30 years of age and are elected directly by the people every six years. In order to guarantee continuity not all senators are elected at the same time. Only one-third of the Senate stands for election every two years, so there will always be enough people with experience in the law-making process. The Senate is presided over by the **vice president** of the USA. Altogether the House of Representatives is composed of 435 members. How many members each state may elect to the House is determined by the size of population. In the first House of Representatives one member represented about 30,000 citizens, today one member represents about 730,000 people. Seven states have only one representative, California has 53. To qualify for election to the House, candidates must be at least 25 years old. They serve a two-year term – theoretically a short term of office but in practice most of the members are re-elected several times.

The primary function of Congress is the enactment of laws. To make a new law, a bill is introduced by a member into one of the chambers. Each house of Congress has the power to introduce legislation on any subject except revenue bills, laws for raising money, which must originate in the House of Representatives. The president may not introduce a bill; he has to find friends who will do this for him. After presentation, the bill is discussed and normally sent on to a committee for detailed examination. The Senate has 16 standing, which means permanent, **committees**, the House of Representatives 22. The members of the committees specialise in specific areas of legislation such as foreign affairs, defence, banking, commerce or agriculture. This is to say, members of Congress acquire special knowledge in one or two areas of policy and as experts advise their colleagues when a new bill which falls into their field of work is presented. When a committee has approved of a bill it is then sent to the floor for open debate. When the debate is ended, the members of the chamber vote either to approve the bill, defeat it, table it – which means setting it aside – or return it to the committee. If a bill is approved, it goes to the other chamber because all bills must be passed by both houses of Congress. Once it has been passed by both chambers, the president signs it and it becomes law. If a bill is vetoed (not signed) by the president it can still become law if it is passed a second time by a two-thirds vote of both houses. The same pattern of separate branches is found in state, county, township and city governments. Each state has a governor as chief executive. Governors often became presidential candidates and some moved on to the vice-presidency or presidency, e. g. Ronald Reagan (was Governor of California), Bill Clinton (Arkansas), and George W. Bush Jr. (Texas).

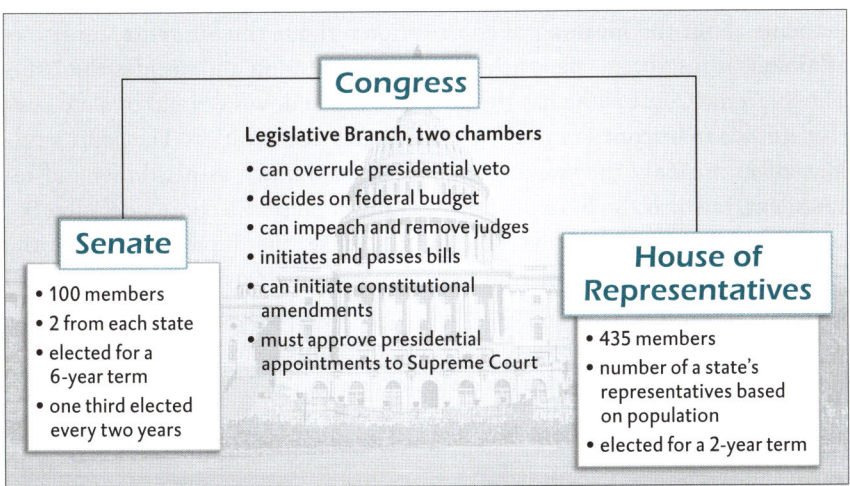

Congress

Legislative Branch, two chambers

- can overrule presidential veto
- decides on federal budget
- can impeach and remove judges
- initiates and passes bills
- can initiate constitutional amendments
- must approve presidential appointments to Supreme Court

Senate

- 100 members
- 2 from each state
- elected for a 6-year term
- one third elected every two years

House of Representatives

- 435 members
- number of a state's representatives based on population
- elected for a 2-year term

The Judiciary Branch

Supreme Court

The Supreme Court of the United States was created by the Judiciary Act of 1789 and consists of justices who are appointed by the president with the advice and consent of the Senate. The number of justices varied in the past, but since 1869 has remained at nine, including a chief justice. In 2005, John Glover Roberts became the 17th **Chief Justice**. Justices are removable only by impeachment. The chief justice presides over all sessions and five judges constitute a quorum to hear a case. There must be a **majority vote** before a decision is made. If a tie exists, the previous decision is upheld. The Supreme Court is the court of last resort for people who believe that lower courts have failed them.

The entrance to the building of the Supreme Court in Washington is inscribed with the motto: "Equal justice under law".

The Supreme Court Justices have the option of whether or not they wish to hear a case. Out of the 7,000 to 8,000 cases appealed each year to the United States Supreme Court, it actually hears about 80 of them. When there are arguments about the meaning of constitutional rights the Supreme Court acts as arbiter, it interprets the articles of the Constitution and decides the issue. The Supreme Court alone has the power to strike down Federal or state laws that it finds to be contrary to the United States Constitution. The court's rulings affect not only the two contesting parties, known as petitioner and respondent, but also the lives of all Americans because the court's decision becomes part of the law of the land. In this sense, the Supreme Court is the guardian of civil liberties in America. The Supreme Court has heard several hundred cases since it was established, some of which had controversial effects on the country's political and social structure. These historic decisions are referred as "**landmark decisions**".

Landmark Decisions

The Supreme Court has often shown its independence of government and Congress influence. While some of its decisions were conservative changes, many were quite radical and often openly criticised by the government. While some decisions did not endure, many shaped American government and the breadth of individual rights:

Marbury v. Madison (1803): This lawsuit is one of the earliest and most celebrated cases. It was fundamentally a legal battle between William Marbury, justice of the peace, and James Madison, secretary of state, about their appointments. What is more important is the fact that for the first time the Supreme Court asserted its authority to oversee the constitution and declare acts of Congress which violate the country's basic law as null and void.

Scott v. Sandford (1857): In the second half of the 19th century, the Court took a few very conservative decisions which obstructed racial integration. The first case concerned Dred Scott, a Missouri slave who had travelled to and worked in "free" states and territories. Scott claimed that he should be entitled to his freedom under the legal principle, "once free, always free". But the Court said blacks could not achieve US citizenship and therefore could not sue in federal courts. The ruling which was a disaster for the blacks in the South helped to precipitate the Civil War and made the creation of the so-called "Jim Crow Laws" possible.

Plessy v. Ferguson (1896): The Court established the "separate but equal" doctrine which permitted racial segregation of public facilities. New regulations, the "Jim Crow Laws", were passed by the state legislatures to establish racial segregation in buses, trains, restaurants, hotels, schools, theatres and even prisons. The "Jim Crow Laws" were used to maintain the unfair treatment and the limitation of the rights of the blacks. Although slavery was abolished the "separate but equal"-practices legitimised by the Plessy v. Ferguson ruling denied the black people in the South equal opportunities in employment and the right to vote.

After World War I the Supreme Court's conservative views met opposition from the liberalism of the New Deal Era. After some of his most important economic recovery programmes were invalidated by the court, President Franklin Roosevelt sought to reform the court by filling vacancies with more liberal justices. Almost 60 years after the Plessy v. Ferguson decision the Supreme Court took a complete 180°-turn and outlawed "separate but equal" facilities because it had become evident that the ruling of 1896 had been used to oppress the African Americans. In 1954, the court issued its landmark desegregation decision and reversed the Plessy v. Ferguson ruling.

Brown v. Board of Education of Topeka (1954): The case name refers to Oliver Brown, an African American, who appealed to the court when his seven-year-old daughter Linda was refused admission to an all-white elementary school in their hometown Topeka, Kansas. The Court ruled that racially separate school facilities in states was a violation of the equal protection clause of the 14th Amendment to the Constitution. This decision spurred the **Civil Rights Movement** and provoked a fundamental change in race relations across America.

Roe v. Wade (1973): The US Supreme Court ruled that states may not ban abortions in the first six months of pregnancy, arguing the 14th Amendment guaranteed a woman's right to end a pregnancy. With this decision, abortion was made legal nationwide.

Texas v. Johnson (1989): The Supreme Court determined that burning the American flag is symbolic speech protected by the First Amendment Right.

District of Columbia v. Heller (2008): The Second Amendment to the United States Constitution protects an individual's right to possess firearms at home for self-defence.

National Federation of Independent Business v. Kathleen Sebelius (2012): The Supreme Court upheld most of President Obama's healthcare law which requires that most Americans buy health insurance.

Riley v. California (2014): The Supreme Court decided that police need a warrant to search data on a suspect's smartphone.

Obergefell v. Hodges (2015): Same-sex marriage is legalised across all 50 states.

Fisher v. University of Texas (2016): Affirmative Action admission (also see page 62) policy is constitutional.

The System of Checks and Balances

Looking at all the varied functions which the American president has, it may seem that his authority is unlimited. However, in the Constitution the Founding Fathers placed restrictions on the president to prevent a dictatorship. The other two branches of government, the Legislative **(Congress)** and the Judiciary **(Supreme Court)**, were assigned responsibilities to control the Executive – and vice versa – so that a delicate system of mutual control developed in which the conflicting interests of the three groups were – and still are – solved by compromises. This elaborate form of government is called the **system of checks and balances**.

Here are a few examples of how the system involves all three branches:

• Congress may impeach and remove the president for "high crimes and misdemeanours".

- Congress may override a presidential veto by a two-thirds majority in both chambers.
- Justices to the Supreme Court are appointed for life by the president, but the Senate must consent to this appointment (or refuse to confirm an appointee).
- The Supreme Court may declare acts of Congress unconstitutional, but Congress may propose an Amendment to the Constitution and thus help to change the Constitution.

Another factor operating as a "balance" is the system of **staggered elections**. The House of Representatives and one-third of the Senate are elected every two years. It often happens that if the president is a Democrat the people vote for a Republican Congress in the elections, and vice versa, which means that a president will have to contend with a majority from the other party in one or both of the two chambers of Congress. This happened to President Barack Obama, who was confronted with a Republican opposition for six years of his presidency. In 2010, two years into Obama's first term, his party lost control in the House of Representatives, in 2014 also in the Senate. Republican Donald Trump was in a much more favourable position to realise his political goals when he became President in 2017 because his party had the majority in both the Senate and the House of Representatives.

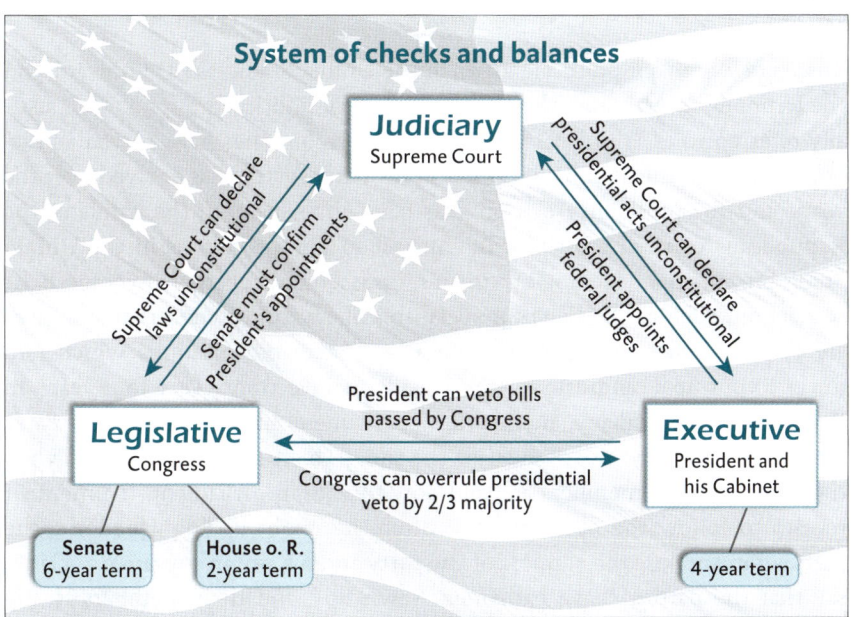

The president, on the other hand, may **veto** laws passed by Congress. The result is that both can keep each other in check, and a stalemate situation ("Patt-Situation") may occur. If Congress decides to be uncooperative, the president faces difficult times indeed because the president cannot govern against the majority in both chambers of Congress. In 2013, the Republican majority in the House of Representatives refused to approve the federal budget of President Barack Obama. As a result, more than 800,000 state employees – about one-third of the federal work force – had to be sent home and services had to be suspended, which meant that attractions such as Yosemite National Park, the Statue of Liberty and Mount Rushmore had to be closed to visitors. The disagreement between Republicans and Democrats has become known as a partial "government shutdown". To overcome a deadlock the president has to shape his policy to find the majority for his plans in Congress. The president can also issue **executive orders** which do not need to be approved by Congress and are legally equal to laws passed by Congress. The authority of the president to issue executive orders is based on the president's executive power defined in the Constitution. Executive orders can be repealed by court decisions or by a two-thirds majority or new laws in Congress.

Political Parties

There are two major political parties in the United States, the Democratic and the Republican. Although there are other minor political groups as well, usually referred to as "third parties", only the two big ones have played an important role on the national level. This two-party system has evolved over the years, and the presidency or Congress have either been in the hands of the Republicans or the Democrats. In contrast to Europe, parties in the United States are not tight ideological organisations bound together by some basic conviction, such as the belief in socialism, liberalism or conservatism. They are basically loose associations of local and state organisations which join forces to put up a candidate for the presidential elections every four years. In Britain and in Germany, members of parliament have to submit to party discipline and party orders most of the time. This means for example when there is a division members are told how to vote in parliament. If a member refuses to follow the party line too often, he might be "punished" by the party whip and lose the support of the party and his seat in parliament. Critics say that the parties "have parliament sewn up", and their members firmly under control. In the United States things are completely different. Senators and members of the House of Representatives have little to do with party discipline, they vote as individuals. They do not owe loyalty to party leaders, they owe loyalty to their local or state electorate and vote accordingly to what the majority of the people in their constituency wishes. The two parties that dominate American politics have a long tradition, which dates back to the **Constitutional Convention** in Philadelphia. When they discussed the role and responsibilities of a central federal government, the delegates were divided into two groups, **Federalists** and **anti-Federalists**.

Democratic Party

The anti-Federalist group had reservations about a strong central government and favoured the autonomy of the states. Its foremost representative was Thomas Jefferson, the author of the **Virginia Bill of Rights**. When he founded the party, he called it "Republican", but his enemies called it "Democratic", a term which they used in the meaning of "demagogic". Born of the anti-Federalist movement, it was, until the beginning of the 20th century, the defender of the states against federal intervention. In this period, Democrats opposed a central bank and protective tariffs. This anti-Federalist tendency reversed itself completely when the Democrat F. D. Roosevelt was elected president (1932). Since then the Democrats have supported central intervention in state affairs. In 1960, Democratic candidate John F. Kennedy won the presidential election beginning the **New Frontier** era that stressed US world responsibilities for peace and economic growth at home.

In the 19th and early 20th century the party gathered its support mainly from farmers, small businessmen, and the professional classes. It attracted voters in the South, in particular, and immigrants of Catholic and Jewish faith in the cities of the North East. Today, Democrats win regularly in the West Coast states and still in the cities of the north and east. They mainly attract liberal whites, women, and voters from minority groups such as African Americans and Hispanics. The party also tends to get votes from low-income and poor families. This view of the Democratic Party as the supporter of the disadvantaged was mainly formed during the presidency of Franklin D. Roosevelt. Roosevelt was elected president in 1932 because the American people thought that President Herbert Hoover did not do enough to fight the economic **Depression**. Within days of taking office, Roosevelt proposed recovery and reform legislation to the US Congress, and soon the government was creating jobs for hundreds of thousands of people. Most of the programmes started during the Depression era were temporary relief measures, but one of the programmes – Social Security – has become an American institu-

President Lyndon B. Johnson signing the Civil Rights Act in 1964

tion. In the 1960s, the Democratic presidents John F. Kennedy and Lyndon B. Johnson not only improved the **civil rights legislation** for the Afro-American population and America's native people, they also established better social assistance programmes. After Kennedy's assassination Johnson became president. In his first State of the Union address, he presented an ambitious programme of domestic legislation to raise the quality of American life and eliminate poverty, calling for an "unconditional war on poverty".

The legislation passed by Congress in 1965 alleviated the lives of many Americans. People living below the poverty line received food stamps. Cheaper accommodation became available for people with low incomes because the state financed the building of houses. Following Johnson's appeal, two social plans, called **Medicaid** and **Medicare**, were elaborated to assist unemployed and elderly people in case of illness and these programmes are important pillars of social security in the United States today. Medicaid pays medical treatment for poor people and is today the nation's largest social-welfare programme. Each state spends up to 22 per cent of its budget to cover costs. Medicare pays about half the costs of the medical bills of people who are over 65, or younger people with disabilities. In view of the fact that there were still too many unemployed Americans who did not qualify for Medicare or Medicaid and who could not afford private health insurance, Democrat Bill Clinton tried to continue along Johnson's lines in 1993. However, the Republican majority in Congress discarded his proposals. During the years of the Bush presidencies (father and son) a reform of the social security system was not on the political agenda. Efforts to reduce the number of American citizens without health insurance were only taken up again when Barack Obama took over as president. In 2010, he succeeded in getting a new law through Congress – the Patient Protection and Affordable Care Act ("ObamaCare"), which provided affordable health care cover. However, it is one of the Trump administration's goals to repeal the act.

Republican Party

The Republican Party, also known as the G.O.P., or **Grand Old Party**, was organized in 1854 as an amalgamation of Whigs with businessmen, workers, and professional people who formerly had called themselves Independent Democrats, Know-Nothings, Barnburners, and Abolitionists. John C. Fremont was the party's first presidential candidate in 1856. Its first successful candidate was Abraham Lincoln, elected in 1860. The party was particularly strong in the period from the Civil War to 1932. In the 1950s to 1970s, Dwight D. Eisenhower (1952, 1956) and Richard Nixon (1968, 1972) each won elections for the Republicans, but both had to work with largely Democratic Congresses.

By and large, the party supports the interests of manufacturing and commercial enterprises, and most of the middle class and the wealthy vote Republican. In 1980, Ronald Reagan, a former movie actor and governor of California, won a landslide election to become the 40th president of the United States. In his inaugural address he outlined a new policy which was named **"Reaganomics"**. He limited government spending and reduced government intervention in the private sector. This attitude reflects the traditional view of the American people that everybody should take care of themselves. **"Self-reliance"** is the keyword and since the days of the pioneers and settlers this has always been regarded as a basic value in American society. Helping the poor had been in the hands of private charity organisations and welfare programmes and a social net comparable to European standards did not exist. Reagan's idea of "back to basics", which on the surface sounded good and sensible, turned into hard times for the sick, handicapped and elderly, because social support programmes, which the Democrats had initiated earlier, were cut or even stopped altogether. Taking up conservative and basic values of the Republican Party, a group of mainly white Americans, among them many women, entered the political arena during the first decade of the 21st century. As their main aim is to protest against more taxes, they are known as the **Tea Party movement**, with reference to the tax protestors in Boston in 1773. The Tea Party activists campaign for a reduction of government spending, especially in the field of social services.

The Differences Between the Parties

Generally speaking, Democrats recruit many of their followers from the less wealthy and cater for their needs, whereas Republicans appeal to those who are strong enough to look after themselves. Therefore, Republicans favour laissez-faire **economics** which means they put more emphasis on private initiative. Everyone should provide for themselves in the first place, before the state steps in. In 1981, President Ronald Reagan summed up this Republican belief: "We are a nation that has a government – not the other way around."

In their platforms, which are published before a presidential election, the Republicans confirm this basic conviction of self-reliance and individual initiative: "We believe that people are the ultimate resource – and that the people, not the government, are the best stewards of our country's God-given natural resources … And this means returning to the people and the states the control that belongs to them. It is the control and the power to make their own decisions about what's best for themselves and their families and communities" (Republican Platform 2016). Consequently, when Republicans such as Reagan (1981–1989) or Bush (George H.: 1989–1993; George W.: 2001–2009) were in government, welfare programmes were reduced substantially – a measure which hit the poorer classes, in particular. On the other hand, Democrats, such as Kennedy (1961–1963), Johnson (1963–1969), Clinton (1993–2001) and Obama (2009–2017) have always seen themselves as advocates of the less fortunate and for minority groups (e. g. African Americans, Hispanics). In their 2016 platform, the Democrats attacked the Republicans for caring only for the wealthy: "Republican governors, legislatures, and their corporate allies have launched attack after attack on workers' fundamental rights to organize and bargain collectively. Too many Americans are living paycheck to paycheck, and hallmarks of a middle-class life – owning a home, having access to affordable and quality childcare, retiring with dignity – feel out of reach. It is no wonder so many Americans feel like the deck is stacked against them". In the field of **foreign policy** Republican presidents tended to follow the doctrine of unilateralism, which means they adhered to the idea that the United States ought to conduct its foreign affairs without the advice or involvement of other nations. For example, President George W. Bush declared the "war on terrorism" (2001) and ordered the invasion of Iraq (2003) without the support of multilateral institutions such as NATO or the United Nations. The Democrats, on the other hand, favour a security strategy which involves a closer cooperation with America's allies.

Party	Origins	Symbol		Colour
Republican Party	formed in 1854	elephant		red
Democratic Party	dating back to the 1790s	donkey		blue

Presidential Elections

The American Electoral System

A **presidential election** takes place every four years. According to the Twenty-Second Amendment to the Constitution the president can be re-elected once. Candidates must be US-born citizens of at least 35 years of age, and they must have been residents of the USA for at least 14 years. More than a year before the actual election a large number of politicians announce their intention to run for the presidency – and a time-consuming and tiring campaign begins. In the past, when there were no jets or helicopters, no modern technologies of communication, aspirants to the office of president needed time to travel around in the country and make themselves known to the electorate. Today, however, things have changed and sceptics argue the campaign lasts much too long and costs too much money. The consequence is that only contenders with sufficient funds or wealthy friends can compete.

Aspirants from the ranks of the two great parties, the Democrats and the Republicans, have to make great efforts to raise money from friends and supporters – if they themselves are not rolling in money. The worrying question then is how much influence will these wealthy contributors have on the future president? There are fears that the costly procedure of electing a US president is not at all democratic, because the "fat cats" (rich people who provide the money) have more influence than the ordinary voter. On the other hand, political analysts argue that the long campaign puts the candidates to a real test. They must prove how much stress they can stand and if they are physically and mentally fit for the most powerful and influential job in the country.

Stages of the US Presidential Elections

Primaries and Caucuses

The first hurdle in the race to the White House is the **primary elections**. For almost two hundred years it was the leaders of the Republican and Democratic parties who picked their presidential candidates. They chose politicians with the best chances to win the election. In an effort to make this nominating process more democratic, however, primaries became common practice in the

20th century. Over a period of months, from January to June in an election year, primary elections are carried out in an increasing number of states. The challengers of the incumbent president make themselves and their political policies known to as large a section of the public as possible. They criticise the president and his party and present themselves as the better alternative. The primary elections are either open to everyone or they are closed, which means that only party members can cast their vote. The voters do not vote for a presidential candidate directly, they choose delegates to the national party conventions. However, voters know which presidential candidate a delegate will support. Another way to test voter sentiment and find the candidate with the most popular appeal, are the **caucuses**. These are informal local party meetings, where party members discuss the chances of individual applicants and express their preferences for a certain candidate.

The primaries serve as a testing ground for the parties and the independent candidates, and although the results are far from being conclusive, the results of one particular day often decide the fate of many aspirants. This special day is **"Super Tuesday"**, a day in March, when primaries take place in a large number of states. It often happens that in view of the results of the primaries on Super Tuesday candidates with little perspective to secure a majority of delegate votes admit their defeat and withdraw from the race for the nomination.

National Party Conventions

After the primaries, in July or August of an election year, the national party conventions of the Republicans and Democrats are held in a city with a large number of Electoral Votes. Here the delegates of the parties nominate the candidate who will represent them at the election in November. These party meetings can best be described as lively spectacles which in many ways resemble the European 'carnival'. The convention hall is brightly decorated, bands play loud music and the state delegates wearing hats in their party and national colours cheer and applaud as prospective candidates are presented. Nominating speeches are delivered to win the support of the delegations assembled for a particular applicant. In the primaries, the delegates told the voters of their state whose nomination they would support. However, during the four days of the national party convention it may happen that the delegates have to vote for somebody else after all. This is the case when none of the candidates gains a majority on the first ballot; then the state delegations are no longer bound to their pledge. As soon as it becomes clear that one aspirant has secured a majority of all delegate votes the remaining votes go to him. This is called "jumping on the bandwagon" – to vote with the majority. In the end the party's candidate for the popular vote in November is supported by an overwhelming majority.

Once the nomination procedure is finished the candidates for the White House deliver an important speech, the **nomination acceptance speech**. In it they address the delegates, the spectators in the hall and the whole American nation in front of their TV sets, summing up the goals of their campaigns and their intentions if they are elected president. One of the most impressive Nomination Acceptance Speeches was held by John F. Kennedy in 1960 when he was nominated candidate for the Democratic Party. Kennedy expressed his policy of the "New Frontier" by reminding the audience of the glorious past of the United States when the pioneers opened up the American continent, relying on their determination and team spirit: "Their motto was not 'every man for himself' – but 'all for the common cause'". Kennedy wanted to revive the pioneer spirit in the American people because he thought that unity and courage were as much needed now as they were in the 19th century: "… we stand today on the edge of a new frontier – the frontier of the 60s – a frontier of unknown opportunities and perils …". The 1960s were the time of the Cold War, and in Kennedy's view the greatest threat to the security of the American nation was the Communist Soviet Union. Social unrest at home also upset the American nation. In order to meet these challenges it was necessary to close ranks and sacrifice personal goals for the common good. On the other hand, new technologies – such as space travel – also opened up new horizons and opportunities. With this great speech Kennedy laid the foundation for his triumph over his rival Republican candidate Richard Nixon, who had served as vice-president under the popular president Dwight D. Eisenhower. Kennedy's victory in the popular vote in November came as a big surprise because he was only 43 years old, and he was a Catholic.

General Election

After their nomination the presidential candidates make every effort to win the votes of the uncommitted electorate. They present themselves at party rallies all over the country, appear on television and in chat shows, trying to appeal to voters of all ages and different backgrounds. The American election day is always the first Tuesday after the first Monday in November. This day was chosen as a compromise to please religious groups who were against Sunday, and business people who did not like Monday. Americans are eligible to vote from the age of 18, but they don't go to the polls in great numbers – only about 50 to 60 per cent actually cast their votes. The majority of Americans watches TV as the results from the precincts (in Britain they are called constituencies) come in on the evening of election day. The American electoral system is similar to the British system as far as it guarantees clear-cut majorities. Whenever a candidate gains the simple majority in a state, he is the winner, he "carries the state", even if he only had a majority of one vote in an electorate of three million. The votes for other candidates or parties are lost. The consequence of such a system, in which the **"winner takes it all"**, is that smaller parties or independent candidates have almost no chances of winning, and that minorities are neglected. On the evening of election day, the American public and the whole world know who will be the next president of the USA, although in the popular vote the American people do not vote for their president directly, they vote for delegates to the Electoral College.

Electoral College

The real presidential election takes place in December when the members of the Electoral College meet in the 50 state capitals and the District of Columbia. The number of electors in each state is equal to its representation in Congress. To give an example, Kansas has six members of the college, because it has two senators and four members in the House of Representatives. This constitutional body was devised when the Constitution was first written. The original idea behind the Electoral College was to have the president elected by unbiased people. But since then things have changed. Political parties developed and competed for power, and today party interests dominate the votes of the electors. Consequently, the meeting of the Electoral College has become a formality, and there is never much suspense about the outcome of the deliberations of the electors, because each state's electors are mandated by the popular vote, which means they have to vote in accordance with the results of the elections which took place in November. The candidate with 270 or more electoral votes is president, regardless of the popular vote.

Inauguration

The final step in the American electoral system is taken in January of the following year when the new president is sworn in by the **Chief Justice**, the highest judge of the **Supreme Court**. This is the oath of office he takes:

"I do solemnly swear (or affirm) that I will faithfully execute the office of president of the United States, and will to the best of my ability, preserve, protect and defend the Constitution of the United States." After this ceremony the new president makes a speech, the **inaugural address**, a keynote speech, in which he outlines his policy.

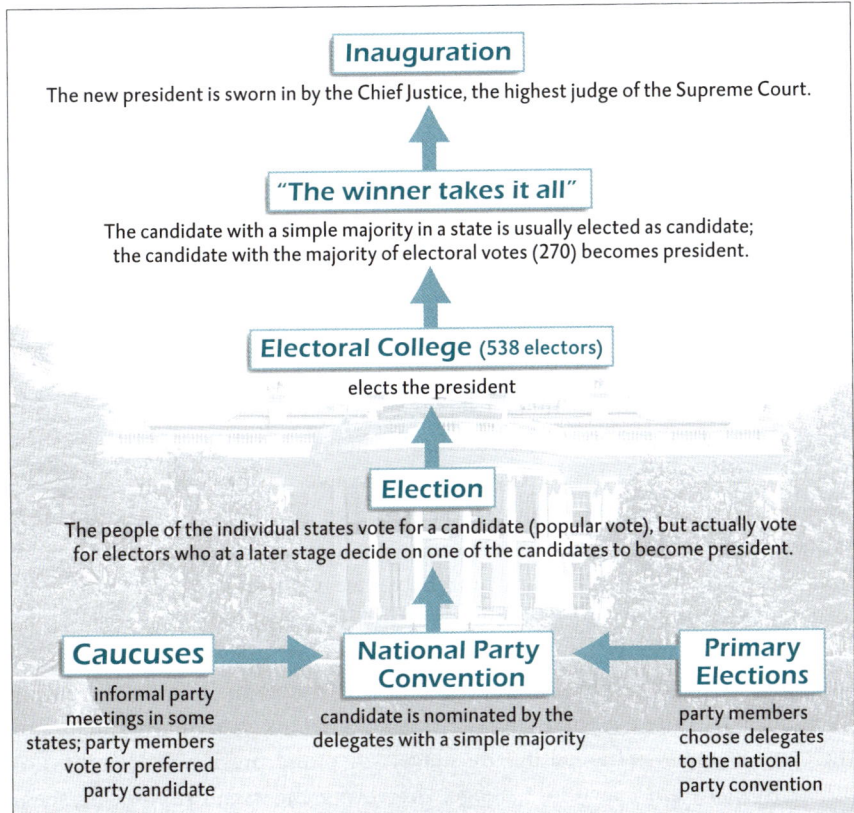

Inauguration
The new president is sworn in by the Chief Justice, the highest judge of the Supreme Court.

"The winner takes it all"
The candidate with a simple majority in a state is usually elected as candidate; the candidate with the majority of electoral votes (270) becomes president.

Electoral College (538 electors)
elects the president

Election
The people of the individual states vote for a candidate (popular vote), but actually vote for electors who at a later stage decide on one of the candidates to become president.

Caucuses
informal party meetings in some states; party members vote for preferred party candidate

National Party Convention
candidate is nominated by the delegates with a simple majority

Primary Elections
party members choose delegates to the national party convention

America's Outdated Electoral College System

The **presidential election of the year 2000** can be seen as a striking example of how unfair the electoral college system may turn out in the end. In 2000, the fight for the presidency was an extremely tight race between Al Gore, who had served as vice-president under Bill Clinton, and his contender, George W. Bush, governor of Texas, and son of former US President George H. W. Bush. According to the stipulations in the Constitution, a candidate needs at least 270 votes in the Electoral College to be elected president. In 2000, the ultimate decision on who would be the next president depended on the result in Florida. Both Gore and Bush needed to win the 25 electoral votes of the Sunshine State to secure a majority in the Electoral College. Although more than 6 million Americans went to vote in Florida, only a mere 537 votes separated the two candidates, with Bush in the lead. As the result was so close the votes were counted again and again. When irregularities were detected lawyers from both sides stepped in arguing for more recounts or trying to stop the process. In the end, it took 36 days until the US Supreme Court put an end to the chaos by ruling that the state-wide recount of votes should stop. Therefore Republican George W. Bush became the 43rd president of the US.

The followers of the Democratic candidate Al Gore were especially bitter about the defeat and many believed they had been robbed of the presidency because although Bush had won the electoral vote, Gore had won the overall popular vote, which means more Americans had voted for Gore than for Bush. However, according to the American electoral system a presidential candidate must win the majority of the votes in the Electoral College, not necessarily the popular vote, because it is the Electoral College which officially appoints the president. Today this system of indirect election of the president which was set up by the Founding Fathers is regarded as undemocratic and hard to understand for the general public. Even if the ordinary American voter was told that the Founding Fathers had to take into consideration that in the nation's early days few Americans were literate, and communication by horseback or sail was slow and unreliable, he would say that the circumstances have changed and that, consequently, the voting system ought to be modified and adapted to our modern world. The "winner-takes-all principle" according to which the candidate who wins the simple majority in the popular vote gets all the electoral votes of this state seems particularly unfair and the controversy was fuelled by the fiercely disputed presidential election of 2000. To many the Electoral College, the voting and counting process seem outmoded, and voices have been raised to abolish this quaint system of electing presidents. Broad discussions about major reforms of a system which was devised in the 18th century by white, slave-owning representatives of the affluent ruling upper class have begun. Political observers believe that the embittered legal battle over election results in Florida in 2000 followed by eight years of Republican George W. Bush as president caused cracks in the American electorate and in the society as a whole. In a country even more divided than 16 years before, the **presidential election of 2016** showed again how unfair the electoral system may turn out in the end: The Democratic Party's candidate, Hillary Clinton, won the popular vote, but not the presidency.

The Presidential Elections of 2008 and 2016

In 2008, a historic change took place: Democrat **Barack Hussein Obama** became the **first African American president** of the United States. The vast majority of African Americans, Latinos and Asians placed their hopes on Obama, securing him and his running mate Joe Biden a landslide victory. The victory of the senator from Chicago was seen as a breakthrough that brought down the last racial barrier in American politics. The first African American arrived at the White House one hundred and forty-five years after Abraham Lincoln had freed blacks from slavery. In addition, after eight years of Republican George W. Bush in power, the nation was ready for a change. Bush had involved the Americans in conflicts in Afghanistan and Iraq and the economy was on the brink of a recession. The majority of the American voters wanted a new government promising a new start. With his slogan "Yes we can", Barack Obama evoked a new confidence in the American people that solutions to the problems the country was confronted with could eventually be found. He promised a withdrawal from Iraq, tax cuts for the middle class, new health insurance and energy programmes as well as support for desperate house owners to help them keep their homes in times of the credit crisis.

During his first term Barack Obama found it hard to fulfil the promises he had made during his 2008 campaign. Although the initial enthusiasm began to die down and realism, coupled with slight disappointment, set in, Obama was voted in for a second term in 2012. President Obama owed his victory to overwhelming support from African Americans, Hispanics and Asian Americans. An analysis made it clear that Republicans could no longer merely rely on votes from the group of well-off Americans mostly of English Protestant ancestry, formerly referred to as WASPs (White Anglo-Saxon Protestants). Their number is decreasing, whereas minority groups are gaining in importance because they constitute an increasing share of the electorate. This analysis, however, did not apply in some respects in the following election.

In 2016, most pollsters predicted a similarly historic outcome as in 2008: that the USA would have its first female president, thus breaking the male stronghold on the presidency. Democrat Hillary Clinton was widely expected to win the race against the Republican candidate Donald Trump, a billionaire real estate tycoon. He seemed an unlikely contender of politically versed Clinton, who had been a senator and had served as Secretary of State under President Barack Obama. Many members of his own party saw Trump as a demagogue, a loudmouth and rather a reality TV character than a politician, too inexperienced to lead the world's most powerful nation. However, with the support especially from white voters Trump managed to out Republican rivals. After both candidates were formally nominated, the Americans had the choice between the oldest candidates ever to enter the presidential race – and both equally unpopular. A bitter campaign set in which was not so much dominated by discussions of politically divergent positions, but personal defamations and mudslinging, with Trump issuing a number of sexist, islamophobic and racist remarks. Clinton, on the other hand, was branded as an un-feeling career politician, who had furthermore put the country's security at risk by sending emails from a private, non-government account. The surprise came for many Americans and for nearly all foreign observers, when Donald Trump won the crucial "**swing states**", in which Hillary Clinton could not muster the same amount of support from traditional Democrat voters (e. g. African Americans, Hispanics) as Barack Obama in 2008 and 2012. Moreover, Trump won votes from the majority of white, male citizens, for example in the Rust Belt, an area especially hard hit by unemployment and economic decline. Analysts described the vote for Trump as "white lash", a reaction to the changing demographic in the USA where white males are in the long run bound to lose their dominant position in American society. In addition, the year-long populist propaganda of far-right groups, such as the Tea Party, had helped to create an aversion against the political establishment in Washington. Therefore, many Americans wanted a new start and voted for the Washington outsider Trump. What also played a crucial role in the campaign was the proliferation of unobjective, often untruthful posts on social media. The bitter and heated election campaign and the victory of Donald Trump did reveal that America is a deeply divided country today. The gap between rich and poor has widened and racism has not been overcome as many had hoped after the election of an African American as president in 2008.

President

Candidate	Popular vote	Percent	Electoral votes
Donald Trump (REP)	61,201,031	47.0 %	306
Hillary Clinton (DEM)	62,523,126	48.0 %	232
Others	6,464,094	5.0 %	0
Electoral votes needed to win: 270			

Data based on: BBC/AP

Senate and House of Representatives (2016)

	Democrats	Republicans	Independents
Senate	46	52	2
House of Representatives	194	241	

Data based on: BBC/AP

Immigration and Population

A Nation of Immigrants

The United States has been called "a nation of immigrants" because of its great ethnic diversity and the fact that only a little bit more than one per cent of its total population of about 328 million are descendants of Native Americans. All others are immigrants or descendants of immigrants. Various ethnic, cultural, and social groups came to America to seek new opportunities and start a new life. English, Scottish, Irish, and Germans, Polish and Russian Jews, Italians, Norwegians, Swedes, Arabs, Chinese, Mexicans, Cubans and many more left their homelands for a number of different reasons – to escape from dictatorships, from religious persecution, unjust class systems, from famine and poverty. On a general level, we can distinguish three periods of immigration to North America: early immigration, European immigration in the 19th century, and immigration today.

Early Immigration
It is usually accepted that early immigration to North America started with the arrival of the first European settlers in the 17th century. It is true that America was not an empty waste of land when they came. More than 10,000 years earlier the very first settlers had arrived on the North American continent from eastern Asia, via Alaska, and in 1492 Columbus had reached the New World. The first permanent European settlement in North America was Jamestown, a colony founded in 1607, and in 1620 it was the arrival of the **Pilgrim Fathers** on their ship **Mayflower** which started the building of the American nation as we know it today.

The Pilgrims, who had fled from religious persecution, began with the colonisation of what were to become the New England states. In the course of time, British, French and Spaniards took possession of great parts of North America. The diverging political and economic interests between Britain and its colonies eventually resulted in the colonists' **War of Independence** and the birth of the United States of America. In the 19th century, immigration on a large scale set in, with tides of newcomers flooding the young nation.

Large-scale Immigration in the 19th Century

The 19th century was the century of European immigration. Hundreds of thousands of small farmers, craftsmen and unskilled workers decided to leave their homelands and look for a better life in the United States, the land of freedom and opportunity. There were **three great waves of immigration** in the 19th century. The first wave between 1820 and 1860 mostly brought immigrants from Great Britain, Ireland, and the German states. During the second wave (1860 to 1890) the British, Irish and German groups were joined by immigrants from Scandinavian countries. During the third wave, from 1890 till 1915, the majority of newcomers were from southern and eastern Europe, from Italy, Austria-Hungary, Poland and Russia. With the outbreak of the First World War and the introduction of quotas in 1921 the uncontrolled inflow came to an end. The great time of immigration was over.

Reasons for Immigration

Although the incentives for emigration were varied, one of the main reasons why people left their homes in the Old World was the **search of a life in peace and freedom**. In the 17th century, the Pilgrims fled from religious oppression and in the 20th century millions sought shelter from tyranny and persecution in Nazi Germany, and later the Communist bloc countries. John F. Kennedy, 35th president of the USA, was proud of America's history as a nation of immigrants: "America has always been a refuge from tyranny". Kennedy, himself a descendant of Irish immigrants, advocated a generous immigration policy. He was convinced that the United States should keep the doors open for refugees from all over the world.

Another driving force behind immigration was the people's hope for **economic improvement**. In the middle of the 19th century the increased use of machinery in agriculture and the mechanisation of the production process in the factories had made thousands of farm workers and craftsmen unemployed. On the other side of the Atlantic, however, the demand for cheap labour had increased at the same time. The Civil War (1861–1865) and the growth of the railroad system spurred industrialisation in the United States. The army needed large amounts of manufactured goods, such as rifles, uniforms and all sorts of supplies. The building of the railroads opened up the vast country, making the transportation of heavy loads over large distances possible. As a consequence, the American industry grew and expanded rapidly, with factories springing up everywhere. Manufacturers needed more and more workers and many of them advertised in European newspapers, even offering to pay the fare for would-be emigrants. Because of the continuous industrialisation, large numbers of immigrants were allowed into the United States to supply the much wanted labour. It was a give and take. However, people also emigrated to America out of sheer desperation, to escape starvation, for example, like over one million Irish in the 1840s when Ireland was hit by the **potato famine**, which cost the lives of over one million people.

Others came because they were **looking for adventure** in a country where there seemed to be no limits imposed by some governing authority, a country where there was room enough for people to lead a life according to their very personal preferences. Still others were attracted by the **lure of nature** – the wilderness possessed a certain magic which led many people to think of America as the new "Garden of Eden". Endless prairies and huge fertile valleys promised excellent conditions for farmers who fled from tiny strips of land in their home country. Thomas Jefferson believed that contact with nature led to a virtuous life. Therefore, he idealized the **yeoman farmer** and his sacred plough.

Once the newcomers had made some progress in their new home country they wrote to family and friends back home to report on their new life. Many immigrants gave glowing accounts of life in the New World, describing their new home country as a classless society with high wages, low prices, good land and a democratic government. "I would not press anyone to come but I will say they cannot provide so comfortable for their families in England as they can here with any given capital … but my earnest wish is, to see all that I love and respect in this land of liberty where … they might enjoy the fruit of their labour …" (John Ingle, from Princeton, Indiana, to England, Aug 28, 1818). Reports like these, together with the propaganda of the steamship lines which promoted their profitable business of transporting the immigrants across the seas, attracted more newcomers. However, there were also those who did not find what they sought and returned to their home countries. It is estimated that during the period 1900–1914, for example, up to one third of immigrants from Europe went back there. This reversal of immigration can also be observed today, as more Mexicans are leaving the United States than migrating into the country. One of the main reasons is their desire to reunite with their families.

The "Huddled Masses"

The millions of poor and suppressed people who sought and found asylum in the New World are often referred to as the "huddled masses". This term is taken from a famous poem by Emma Lazarus, "The New Colossus", which is inscribed on a tablet inside the pedestal of the **Statue of Liberty**, the majestic copper figure at the entry to New York Harbour.

In 1876, Emma Lazarus wrote her poem in commemoration of the hundredth anniversary of American independence, and the French government presented an enormous statue as a gift to the United States symbolizing the liberty granted in both countries. The sculpture, standing 93 m high from ground level to torch, was created by the French sculptor Frederic Auguste Bartholdi. The figure wears a crown with spikes, representing the continents, and in her left hand carries a tablet bearing the inscription "July 4, 1776", the date on which the **Declaration of Independence** was proclaimed. On October 28, 1886, the statue was erected in the harbour of New York, and since then refugees have been welcomed to their new home country by the sight of the imposing statue holding a torch into the air – which explains its full name: "Liberty Enlightening the World".

Journey across the Sea and Arrival in the New World

In the 1890s, the fare from Bremen to New York, cost the mostly poor emigrants an enormous sum. But their hopes and their dreams spurred them on and gave them the strength to put up with the sometimes dangerous and always uncomfortable journey across the Atlantic. On the great steamships of the White Star and Cunard shipping lines the steerage passengers were jammed together below deck for the two-week crossing, often enduring almost unbearable conditions.

New York was the main entry point for mass immigration by sea. The great steamships arrived here with their loads of hopeful immigrants.

Mulberry Street in "Little Italy", New York City, around 1900

Many newcomers stayed in New York, making it into the "City of the World (for all races are here, all the lands of the earth make contributions here)"– in the words of the American poet Walt Whitman –, a symbol of immigrant enterprise and ethnic integration. Most of the immigrants, however, had a difficult start in New York. The cheapest accommodation was available in the city's Lower East Side, where families often crammed into tiny rooms without ventilation, daylight or running water. Earning one's living was hard, for example in the sweatshop factories of the textile industry. Nathaniel Hawthorne once wrote: "In this republican country, amid the fluctuating waves of our social life, somebody is always at drowning point."

When towards the end of the 19th century the tide of immigration from southern and eastern Europe began to flood the country, the "older" immigrants from northern Europe were calling for restrictions to bar the newcomers whom they looked down upon. In response to this call for restrictions, the first official federal immigration centre was opened at **Ellis Island** in 1892. Until 1954, for more than 12 million men, women and children who were allowed into the country the processing centre became "The Isle of Hope". Each week, thousands of people had to go through the terrifying immigration routine – medical inspection and psychological examination. Immigrants who showed any signs of illness, especially contagious diseases, and "politically doubtful characters" or convicts were sent back home on the next

Immigrants on Ellis Island (1902)

boat. For these few – about 2 per cent – Ellis Island turned into "The Isle of Tears". Today the place where about 40 per cent of the ancestors of today's Americans arrived in the New World has been turned into a museum.

Germans in America

The first German immigrants arrived in America in the early 17th century. Most Germans settled in Pennsylvania and made Germantown an important place for handicraft. Other Germans stayed in New York or moved to New Jersey (New Brunswick). The German Baron Friedrich Wilhelm von Steuben, for example, helped to form a disciplined army for General Washington to win the War of Independence.

Most German immigrants, about six million, arrived in the United States between 1820 and 1916. The reasons for emigration were, for example, crop failure and famine, poverty, social upheaval and political persecution. Those who had sold their possessions in Germany came with enough money to buy farms from Americans who were about to move further west. Many Germans also moved to cities, particularly New York, St. Louis, Chicago and Cincinnati. The unskilled workers took any job available, but a high number of German immigrants were able to practise the craft they had learned back home: tailoring, baking, bookbinding, making furniture. Very soon and very quickly German immigrants were able to raise their standard of living, making German Americans the most successful of all non-English speaking immigrants by World War I. Of particular importance were German contributions in the fields of business, science, engineering, music and education. Famous Americans with German roots were, for example, John Jacob Astor (1763–1848, businessman and investor), Carl Schurz (1829–1906, army general in the Civil War, and the first German-born American elected to the United States Senate), Henry John Heinz (1844–1919, founder of the Heinz Company, famous for its ketchup), and William Edward Boeing (1881–1956, founder of the Boeing Company).

However, after the US had declared war against Germany in 1917, anti-German sentiment developed across the nation. Being anti-German became a way of showing patriotism for the American war effort. People of German descent were suspected of being traitors, German books were censored, German-language magazines and newspapers stopped publishing and schools banned teaching German. Towns and cities re-named streets which had German names. The community of New Berlin in Ohio, for example, changed its name to North Canton, which it has kept ever since. German Americans also anglicised their surnames (e. g. "Müller" became "Miller", "Schmidt" became "Smith"), thus removing visible traces of German ancestry.

The American Dream

"From rags to riches, from dishwasher to millionaire" – the hope of self-improvement and success is traditionally expressed in the term "American Dream". For many it has been a vision, an aspiration – and for others an illusion. Some of the immigrants who emigrated to the United States believed that in the "the land of promise" the streets would be paved with gold. The more realistic immigrants, however, simply hoped for a better life. They firmly believed that in America personal success was possible and within reach of each individual because of the social, economic and political conditions for hard-working people. The American Dream implies **liberty, justice** and the **pursuit of happiness**, as expressed in the American Declaration of Independence of 1776.

The belief and trust in personal achievement based on private initiative has become the foundation of American society. However, this dream of a democratic and prosperous society guaranteeing "liberty and justice for all" has not yet been achieved for all groups in America. In the 1960s, in his famous speech "I have a dream" Martin Luther King referred to the ideal of equality as "a dream deeply rooted in the American Dream" and expressed his optimism that it would come true for black people too. In 1997, President Clinton reminded the American people to continue striving for the realisation of the American Dream for all Americans: "Martin Luther King's dream was the American Dream."

However, this optimistic outlook has almost vanished in the last two decades as the pursuit of that dream of happiness and prosperity has become much harder for many Americans. Worse still, instead of making it to the top or at least leading a decent life, many people are left without a job, struggling for survival. They see their future, their American Dream, destroyed because of racism, or the technological advances of automation or the negative effects of globalisation. An increasing number of white workers blame the influx of immigrants, especially from Latin America, who, they argue, take away their jobs and opportunities. This is why Republicans advocate more effective immigration controls, especially between the US and Mexico, by building an "impenetrable wall" along the 3200 km-long southern border to replace the various types of fences and structures which already exist.

The Frontier

In the view of the settlers, the "**frontier**" was the dividing line between the white settlements and, as they saw it, the free unoccupied land beyond. It was the border country between civilisation and "the wilderness". The early colonists had built their homes and cities on the east coast, but very soon adventurers like Daniel Boone began to explore and open up new lands outside the boundaries, first north and then west, eventually to the Pacific coast. In 1803, President Thomas Jefferson ordered an expedition led by Meriwether Lewis and William Clark to trace the Mississippi River to its source and to find the best way to the Pacific Ocean. The report of the successful expedition, published in 1814, informed the American public about the potential of the territories in the **Far West**.

Fifty years later, after the end of the **Civil War** in 1865, the move west began, pushing the frontier further and further into unknown territory. The driving forces behind the **westward movement** were the quest for cheap land and natural resources, economic opportunities, better living conditions for families and self-improvement. The first whites to move into the unknown were the hunters and **trappers**, followed by the backwoods settlers who were half hunters, half farmers. Then came the **farmers**, many of them optimistic and idealistic immigrants from Europe, who were drawn into the wilderness by the abundance of land. The main lines of migration came from the East and South. Important routes, like the Santa Fe Trail and the Oregon Trail, both of which followed old Indian paths, opened new lands to adventurous and daring pioneers. A favourite starting point was the town of Independence in Missouri. Many pioneers set out from there in their wagons on a 3,000 km overland route which took them down the Missouri River, through the **Great Plains** across the Rocky Mountains and finally into Oregon. People took time in migrating to the West, pausing for a year or more in several places before reaching their final destination. When settle-

Family with their covered wagon during the Great Western Migration, 1866

ments eventually grew in size and villages and towns developed, the third wave of the pioneer movement arrived. Merchants, doctors, bankers and lawyers came to provide services to the growing population.

The building of a **system of railroad lines** across the continent and the discovery of **gold in California** played an important part in the settlement of the Far West. When in 1848 James Marshall found nuggets of gold in a river in northern California, the news spread like wildfire, and more than 100,000 miners poured into the country. Some prospectors struck it rich, others were less lucky, but eventually stayed in the new land. In 1859, reports of gold and silver discoveries in Colorado and Nevada caused an influx of fortune hunters. Realising the overall importance of a reliable and efficient transport system, the American government encouraged railway companies to lay tracks across the United States by giving them free land and financial support. The Union Pacific Railroad started in the east, the Pacific Railroad in the west, in California.

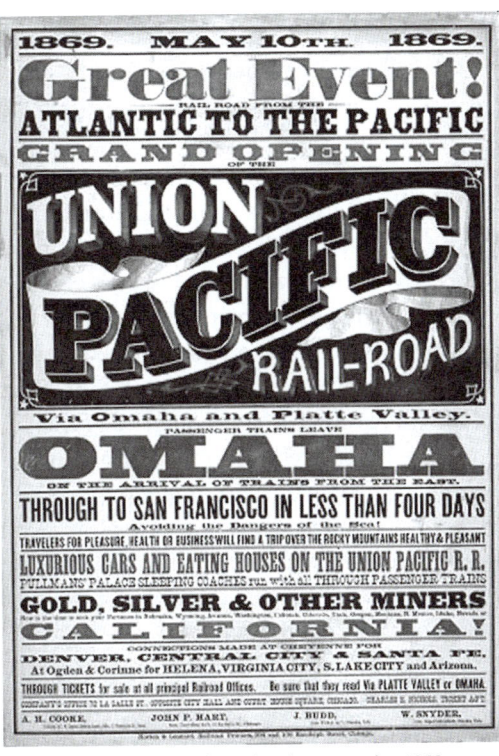

Poster for the Union Pacific Railroad opening-day, 1869

When both lines met in Promontory in Utah, the first transcontinental railway line was completed. Between 1870 and 1900, the whites had settled more land than in the 150 years before, completing the conquest of the West, America's frontier.

The Pioneering Spirit

Frederick Jackson Turner was among the first American historians to explain how deeply the conquest of the frontier influenced the development of the American nation and the character of its people. Ever since the initial colonisation of the continent, the American people have been a "people in motion" and mobility has become a unique trait that distinguishes Americans from Europeans. Charles Dickens saw the West as "peopled by a vast human army, consisting of people who had dedicated their lives to leaving home after home behind."

Since the days of the frontier movement Americans have always placed high value on independence, self-confidence and individualism – the virtues of pioneer life. When seen from the positive side, the pioneering spirit has promoted people's ability to overcome difficulties through private initiative and invention. On the other hand, however, in many heroic frontier stories and Hollywood Western movies the pioneers' individualism was reduced to a frequent use of guns and "trigger-happy gunmen" set the scene. These colour-ful pageants paint a distorted picture of the past because in reality the pion-eers made little use of rifles and revolvers – most of them were farmers and homesteaders who were inexperienced in the handling of weapons. However, the **glorification of the frontier spirit** led to a culture where firearms were regarded as symbols of freedom. Not surprisingly, America's gun laws are more permissive than in any other nation and weapons can be bought fairly easily. The consequences of this liberal way with firearms are evident: When-ever there are lethal shootings in American schools, for example, sensible people question the individual's right to purchase and carry a gun and liberal politicians call for stricter gun control. Up to now, however, all efforts have been squashed by the powerful National Rifle Association and its supporters.

The Fate of the Native Americans

The conquest of the West was a triumph for the independent, optimistic, hard-working settlers, and a tragedy for the continent's original inhabitants, the Native Americans. The frontier movement ended in a genocide of the native people of America, diminishing their population to a mere 248,000 in 1890 through fighting, disease and starvation. In 2010, the United States officially apologised "for the many instances of violence, maltreatment, and neglect inflicted on Native Peoples by citizens of the United States".

In the beginning, the relationship between the first Europeans and the In-dians was mainly friendly, and the settlers depended on the help of the na-tives to survive in a hostile environment. However, the situation changed as more and more "sod-busters" – the farmers who cleared the land and started their farms in the wilderness – tracked west and occupied Indian territory. They drove the natives relentlessly off the land of their ancestors, killing thousands who were unwilling to make room and be moved into reserva-tions, usually barren, infertile grounds the whites did not want. To justify the cleansing of the Indians the concept of "Manifest Destiny" was propagated, according to which it was the Godly mission of the white man to conquer the wilderness and civilise the "inferior and culturally primitive savages".

The myth of "Manifest Destiny" helped push waves of American settlers westward to the Pacific, displacing native peoples and devastating their culture and traditional way of life. The resistance the Indians put up against the white invaders was weak, as they were not united among themselves and tribal warfare was frequent. The greatest Indian victory was won in 1876 when Sioux warriors defeated and annihilated the 7th Cavalry commanded by the over-ambitious and reckless George Armstrong Custer at Little Bighorn. Most of the time, however, Indian uprisings, which were often protests against the fact that the whites had broken earlier treaties or promises, were crushed with utter brutality during the Indian wars in the second half of the 19th century. Subsequent federal government Indian policies always safeguarded the interests of the whites and neglected those of the original inhabitants. Laws like the General Allotment Act of 1887, also called Dawes Act, facilitated the acquisition of land for the white settlers and the Indians were moved into ever smaller reservations.

In the 20th century, the Indian policy of the government aimed at the integration of Native Americans into urban centres, thus hastening the termination, and extinction, of tribes. These efforts at forced assimilation ("termination policy") were not successful, however, and given up in the 1960s by the Johnson administration. Since the 1970s, after Indian protestors had occupied Alcatraz Island in San Francisco Bay to alarm the public about the misery of the disadvantaged native population, a new policy, called "self-determination", has been in effect. It has kept the protective role of the federal government – providing Native Americans with education and various forms of support – and has increased the participation of the tribes in important areas of local government.

About one-third of today's 2.9 million Native Americans live in the states of California, Arizona and Oklahoma. Where natural resources (coal, oil, natu-

Reviving Native American heritage: Powwow in northern Wisconsin

ral gas or uranium) are found, the Indians lease out exploitation rights to white companies, others live from farming or tourism. Some tribes run casinos, the profits of which go back to the members. The urban Indians try to survive in the cities accepting all sorts of menial jobs. The living conditions of the majority of Native Americans are still appalling, despite efforts of the **Department of Housing and Urban Development** (HUD). Unemployment, alcoholism and frequent disease are constant threats, which altogether make the Native Americans the poorest ethnic group in the USA. In spite of all this there is a silver lining on the horizon. On many reservations the Native Americans make efforts to revive their tribal heritage, their languages and religious ceremonies and restore in their children the pride of belonging to the continent's original inhabitants.

20th Century Immigration and Newcomers Today

In the early days of mass immigration, most newcomers were welcomed because they contributed to the success of the new-born nation that desperately needed more strong hands to conquer its vast territory and build its economy. Today, Americans are divided in their attitude towards immigration. According to a recent poll of the Pew Research Center, the population is evenly split on the question whether growing immigration is good or bad for the country, with positive attitudes to immigration having increased in the last decade.

Because of the influx of non-European immigrants **America's ethnic structure** has already changed. In the 21st century the population of the United States will continue to grow increasingly diverse, with Asia and Central America remaining the major sources of immigration. Today, the Hispanic population has already outnumbered the black population. By 2050, according to estimates, approximately 46 per cent of the population in the United States will be Whites, 30 per cent Hispanic, 15 per cent African-American, and 9 per cent Asian.

Hispanic Immigration

By 1910 the great period of immigration was over, and after the two world wars, Congress passed new and stricter immigration laws with set quotas for each country which de facto closed the doors to the United States. It took many years before immigrants were admitted again in greater numbers. Fifteen years after the end of World War II, in the 1960s, the US government changed its immigration policy. The government dropped ethnically based quotas on immigration and favoured immigration from Third World nations. Since then the number of non-European immigrants has risen considerably. From the 1960s onwards would-be entrants came mainly from Asia and from the countries south of the US border.

In 1950, fewer than four million US residents were Hispanics – immigrants from Spanish-speaking countries such as Cuba, Mexico, or Puerto Rico. Today that number is about 57 million (about 17 per cent of the US population), which makes the Hispanic community in the United States the second largest in the world – after Mexico. Hispanics, also called Latino Americans, represent the fastest-growing population group. Between 2000 and 2010, their number increased by 43 per cent compared to merely 5 per cent of the non-Hispanic population. Large communities can be found in border states to Mexico like California, Texas, Arizona and also in southern Florida. However, in recent years Latinos have spread into all areas of the US. In many places, such as Miami or East Los Angeles, they dominate the population. The driving force behind this growth is no longer immigration, but an increased number of births in the country. The increase in this section of the US population has considerable consequences on the country's social and political structure. Traditionally, Hispanics mainly support the Democratic Party and thus contribute immensely to the Democratic electorate.

Asian Immigration

The Chinese were the first ethnic group to be affected by immigration laws towards the end of the 19th century. They had come to the US in such large numbers that people in America feared the Chinese would take away jobs. Prejudice against Asians and fear of the so-called "yellow peril" were so strong that anti-Chinese riots broke out in 1880. Two years later Congress passed the first of the Chinese Exclusion Acts which barred Chinese "coolies" ('Hilfsarbeiter') from immigration to the United States and excluded Chinese from naturalisation. It took until 1943 before the laws that kept out Chinese immigrants were repealed, and after the Immigration and Nationality Act of 1952 immigration from Asia increased rapidly. In the 1970s, many Asian immigrants came as refugees after the end of the Vietnam War. Today about 18 million people are of Asian descent. Many of them live in the big cities of Los Angeles, New York and San Francisco. More recently, Las Vegas and Atlanta have become favourite destinations, too. As to the socio-economic standing of Asian immigrants, the same pattern as in Britain can be observed. Asians are among the most successful of all immigrant groups. They have a higher income than many other ethnic groups, and large numbers of their children study at the best US universities as undergraduate and postgraduate students.

Illegal Immigration

The number of illegal immigrants in the United States has increased tremendously in the last decades but stabilized in the last few years. Most illegal immigrants are Mexicans who come to the US by crossing the Rio Grande. About 11.5 million foreigners live in the US today without the necessary documents. A considerable number enter the country legally with a student, tourist, or business visa. However, many do not leave when their visas expire but stay on. Approximately two-thirds of illegal immigrants have been in the US for at least ten years. It is not difficult for them to find a job because many employers are looking for cheap labour to keep wage costs down. Illegal immigrants work in private homes as servants, gardeners, child minders, nurses,

US-Mexican border fence near El Paso

or on building sites and in agriculture – all in all in occupations which require little formal education or training and demand no official licence. In addition, many temporary or migrant workers work on a seasonal basis harvesting crops in the fields of California. However, more and more illegal aliens are no longer satisfied with menial jobs. Many have acquired qualifications and apply for better-paid jobs such as carpenters, bricklayers and machine operators. This is why local citizens see the competition of the immigrants as a threat to their own chances on the job market. It is the increase in illegal immigration which worries ordinary people and which has caused social tension between Americans and illegal immigrants. Reacting to the growing public concern politicians from both parties are working towards tightening the regulations under which immigrants are admitted in order to cut down the number of newcomers in general and of unauthorised arrivals in particular. The Secure Fence Act of 2006 was one of the measures of the US administration to make borders more secure. After his re-election in 2012, President Obama promised an overall reform of the immigration system, but his proposals were blocked by the Republicans. To overcome the resistance he announced a set of executive actions in 2014. These allow up to an estimated 45 per cent of undocumented immigrants to legally stay and work in the United States. In June 2016, however, the Supreme Court was deadlocked regarding the question whether Obama's executive actions could be implemented or not. So the hopes of millions of illegal immigrants on immigration reform were shattered again and the issue of legalisation remains unresolved.

Melting Pot or Salad Bowl?

Traditionally, the United States has been regarded as a melting pot where immigrants from many different cultures, races, and religions have been assimilated and moulded into "the first universal nation". People no longer felt German, Italian, Polish or Irish – they thought of themselves as Americans, as members of a truly multicultural society. During the 19th century, when most immigrants came from Europe, assimilation was not difficult because the newcomers did not look much different and were able to blend in quite easily. However, two factors have brought about a change so that now more and more cracks in the melting pot are being discovered. First of all, since the shift in US immigration policy in the late 1960s, when the government dropped ethnically based quotas on immigration, the number of non-white immigrants has risen considerably. Sociologists have described this process as the "browning of America". Secondly, not all non-European immigrants wish to wholly blend into American culture as they do not want to discard their customs and traditions. They take pride in their ethnic heritage and wish to pass it on to their children, and – above all – they want to keep their mother tongue. In many parts of the south-western and south-eastern United States English already plays a secondary role because most newcomers are keeping to their Spanish. In Florida and California non-melting ten-

Naturalisation ceremony for new U.S. citizens

dencies are most obvious. Latinos have their own theatres, cinemas, television channels, restaurants and bars.

Every year more than one million immigrants want to become Americans and apply for naturalisation. Having passed a test on the basics of American citizenship, history and culture, they swear allegiance to the flag. However, the old view of the nation as a melting pot is no longer true and many people are beginning to refer to it as a myth. Multiculturalists – people who are convinced of the advantages of a multicultural society – have given up using the term "melting pot" because of the word's underlying meaning of "enforced assimilation". Today most people prefer to see the United States as a **salad bowl**, or a fruit salad – a combination of many cultures, living and working together, each distinct and separate. The ingredients can still clearly be identified, which means the immigrant groups have kept their ethnicity. Other sociologists prefer the symbol of a mosaic or a tapestry: each colour is distinct and adds to the overall beauty of the object. These metaphors suggest that it is acceptable to keep one's differences and still be part of the overall society. The majority of the immigrants tried very hard to reach the land of their dreams, some even had to sacrifice their lives. Once they are admitted, the question is not so much as whether to integrate completely into American society and adopt the American way of life as whether to keep one's ethnic identity. Most important is that the immigrants assimilate enough, e.g. by learning the language to take full advantage of the possibilities which their new homeland offers. On the other hand, immigrants from all parts of the world have given America its cultural diversity that has made it a vibrant nation.

The Civil Rights Movement in the USA

What is the Civil Rights Movement?

When we talk about the Civil Rights Movement in the United States, we refer to the protests against racial segregation and discrimination of blacks in the Deep South. In the 1950s and 1960s the fight for equal and fair treatment became an important issue. Through the leadership of the Baptist minister **Martin Luther King** the campaign for equality gained momentum and was turned into a mass movement. King's methods of **non-violent direct action** (the organisation of boycotts, sit-ins, demonstrations and protest marches) were increasingly supported not only by black but also by white Americans. The Civil Rights Movement achieved two great victories with the passage of the **Civil Rights Act** of 1964 and the **Voting Rights Act** of 1965, which recognised black Americans as equal citizens and secured their right to vote.

    Civil rights are the freedoms and privileges given to a citizen of a country; among these are the rights to political and social freedom and job equality irrespective of a person's sex, race or religion. **Human rights**, on the other hand, are the rights belonging fundamentally to all people, i. e. the basic freedoms that all human beings should have (e. g. the right of life, the right to say what you think or to travel freely). Although the Civil Rights Movement will mainly be connected with the name of Martin Luther King, the struggle for the emancipation of black Americans has a long tradition.

The Beginnings of Slavery and Segregation

For hundreds of years blacks in America were called "negroes". Then, from the 1960s, they were referred to as "blacks" or "black Americans", but today they themselves prefer the term **African Americans** to remind of their origin and the fact that they did not come to America of their own free will, but, in the words of John F. Kennedy, "were bought and sold and had no choice".

Voyage into Slavery

In the early 17th century the slave trade between the African and the American continent began. British vessels transported natives from Africa's west coast to the Caribbean and the American South where they were sold as slaves to work on the cotton, tobacco and sugar plantations. Not all of the captured black people survived the journey on the tightly packed ships. The ones who could not endure the appalling conditions on the ships were thrown overboard. "Sharks had learnt that following the slave ships was the way to grow fat", Malcolm X said later. By the time the United States was founded, slavery was practised in all of the 13 states. Although the Declaration of Independence clearly stated that "all men are created equal", the principle of equality did not include blacks, as the slaves were not regarded as "men" or "human beings" nor were they citizens of the United States. They were seen as a welcome source of cheap labour and had contributed greatly to the wealth of the South. So slavery was an important economic factor and influential plantation and slave owners were not willing to renounce that privilege.

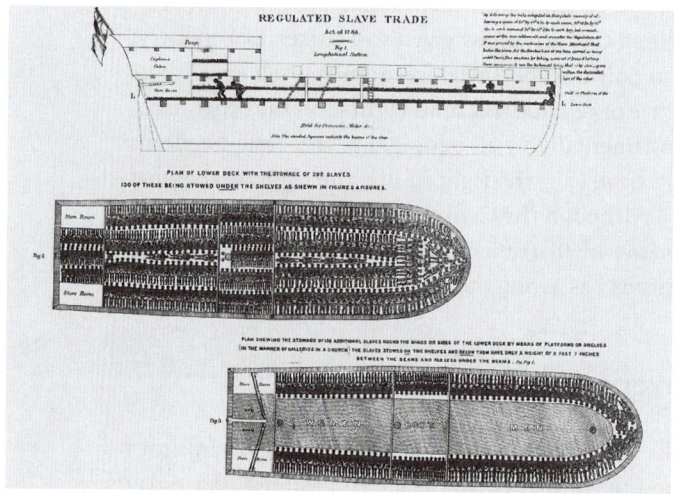

Slave traders transported slaves from the west coast of Africa to the American South where they were sold to work on the plantations. The slaves were packed tightly below deck and kept in chains day and night. Those who died during the sea passage were thrown overboard.

North versus South: Free at last?

In the early 19th century slavery and the treatment of blacks as second-class human beings came under heavy criticism. Anti-slavery associations were formed, which raised moral questions about slavery and advocated the abolition of this inhumanity. The argument between the North and the South about this question contributed to the outbreak of the **American Civil War**

(1861–1865), although, in reality, the war was essentially about economic and political power. The rural South believed in its right to leave the Union ("secession") and wanted to keep slavery as its agriculture depended to a large extent on slave labour. The growing industries in the North, on the other hand, were able to recruit enough workers from the ranks of the masses of European immigrants who were arriving from across the Atlantic. As a result of the victory of the Northern states in the conflict slavery was finally abolished. President Lincoln's 1863 **Emancipation Proclamation** declared the slaves free. The **Thirteenth Amendment** (1865) to the US Constitution abolished slavery and the **Fourteenth Amendment** (1868) extended US citizenship to all former slaves.

Slavery is replaced by Segregation

Despite these legal achievements, the situation of the black Americans in the South did not change for the better and racial discrimination continued. Slavery was followed by segregation of whites and blacks, with "separate but equal" facilities. That means that businesses and public accommodations were segregated according to race. In buses, trains, restaurants, hotels, schools, theatres and even jails there were special sections reserved for whites and others for blacks, so that both groups would not meet and mix. The highest court of the country, the Supreme Court, legitimised in a decision of 1896 the practice of "separate but equal" facilities. As a matter of fact, more and more rules were introduced to enforce segregation. The so-called **"Jim Crow Laws"** were passed, officially for the protection of the blacks, but in reality the regulations were used to maintain the unfair treatment and the limitation of the rights of the black part of the population. Originally, "Jim Crow" was the name of a song-and-dance act, but the expression came to be used as an insulting name for blacks in general. Because of the "Jim Crow" practices, black people in the South were denied equal opportunities in employment and, above all, the right to vote. Consequently, they remained the powerless victims of discrimination.

Winds of Change after World War II

During the first half of the 20th century little progress was made in the fight for racial equality, but the winds of change began to blow after the end of World War II. In the North, blacks could acquire a decent living and from their economic achievements they drew enough confidence to press for their full rights as US citizens. Internationally, the United States had committed itself to the defence of freedom and democracy for all mankind, fighting in World War II against Nazi Germany and denouncing the disregard of human rights in the Communist bloc. Liberal whites criticised the American hypocrisy, pointing to the contradiction between what the US required from others and what it practised at home. In 1948, President Harry S. Truman ordered the desegregation of the armed forces, in view of the fact that blacks had fought bravely as US soldiers in the war.

In 1954, the United States Supreme Court took a historic decision. In the legal case "Oliver **Brown versus Board of Education** of Topeka, Kansas", the Supreme Court decided unanimously on May 17, 1954, that the "separate but equal" concept was unconstitutional, thus overthrowing its ruling of 1896. This decision not only paved the way for school desegregation but also marks the beginning of a mass movement of blacks, and white sympathisers to end the segregationist practises and racial inequalities across the nation and particularly in the South.

Martin Luther King and the Civil Rights Movement

Montgomery Bus Boycott

It was a small incident in Montgomery, Alabama, which triggered off a mass protest and gave the Civil Rights Movement new impetus. On a cold December evening in 1955, 42-year-old **Rosa Parks**, who worked as a seamstress in a factory, was on her way home from work riding on a bus. According to the strict segregation rules of the Montgomery City Bus Lines black passengers had to sit in the back and had to give up their seats if the white section in the front of the bus became occupied. Ms Parks was sitting in the first row of the rear section designated for blacks. It was a busy day and when the white section of the bus was filled, the driver ordered Ms Parks to give up her seat for a white man. The tired woman was fed up with being treated like a second-class citizen, so she refused and was arrested. The news of her ar-

Rosa Parks and Martin Luther King (around 1955)

rest aroused the leaders of the black community to action. They met at Dexter Avenue Baptist Church to discuss the issue. Among them was a young minister, **Martin Luther King Jr.**, who had been pastor in Montgomery for little more than a year. It was agreed to start a bus boycott in protest against segregated seating on the city buses. The boycott eventually lasted much longer than anyone had expected – 381 days – and the bus company lost more than half of its income. Eight months later, the Supreme Court decided that bus segregation violated the constitution. Because of the non-violent way he had conducted the boycott, Martin Luther King had in little more than a year become one of the nation's most remarkable leaders of the Civil Rights Movement.

The March on Washington
On August 28, 1963, King led a march on Washington to commemorate the signing of the Emancipation Proclamation by Abraham Lincoln during the

Civil War in 1863. 100 years had passed since slavery was abolished, but blacks still did not enjoy the same rights as whites. The march culminated in a mass demonstration in the Mall between the Lincoln Memorial and the Washington Monument. In front of a crowd of more than 250,000 people, including about 60,000 whites, King delivered one of the greatest speeches in American history, his famous "I Have a Dream" speech.

Civil rights and union leaders on the March on Washington in 1963

"I Have a Dream"
In his address, Martin Luther King referred to the words of the **Declaration of Independence** of 1776: "We hold these truths to be self-evident, that all men are created equal". By reminding his listeners of the principles laid down by the Founding Fathers he demanded the delivery of those promises: citizenship rights for the black Americans, justice, equality and freedom. King was optimistic that whites and blacks would one day be able to live together in peace, mutual respect and understanding. In his speech he conveyed his firm conviction that racial integration was the overall goal of the Civil Rights

Movement and he expressed his hopes of a **colour-blind America** where people would not be judged "by the colour of their skin but by the content of their character". Martin Luther King encouraged his listeners to keep up their spirits in spite of the frustrations of everyday life, despite the discrepancies between the ideal of the "land of the free" and the humiliating inequalities blacks were still confronted with.

Martin Luther King was one of the most powerful and skilful orators of the Civil Rights Movement. With his usage of poetic language ("mountain of despair"), his biblical phraseology ("every valley shall be exalted"), his repetition of keywords and key phrases ("I have a dream") and parallel sentence structures he deeply impressed his audience. As a trained and experienced preacher he used elements of a sermon, encouraging the participation of his listeners whom he addressed as "friends". King had prepared his speech in writing but as he was speaking he himself became so emotional and cheered by the immediate response of his audience that he improvised great parts of his speech. Still today "I Have a Dream" has retained all its vigour and freshness: "[…] I say to you today, my friends, so even though we face the difficulties of today and tomorrow, I still have a dream. It is a dream deeply rooted in the American dream."

On April 4, 1968, Martin Luther King was assassinated in a motel in Memphis. These words from a spiritual song which he had quoted in his address "I Have a Dream" are carved on his tombstone: "At last, free at last, thank God Almighty, I'm free at last."

King's Method of Non-violent Resistance

Influenced by his studies of the successful methods applied by Mahatma Gandhi and his Christian convictions as a clergyman Martin Luther King firmly believed in **non-violent action**. With demonstrations, sit-in campaigns and marches he wanted to make white Americans aware of the failure to extend civil rights to the black part of the population. The lethargic response from the whites and the slow progress in the improvement of the living conditions caused younger blacks to become impatient and aggressive. Martin Luther King's tactics of non-violent resistance and civil disobedience were heavily attacked as being too lenient and too soft. One of the most outspoken critics was Malcolm X of the Black Power Movement.

The Militant Black Power Movement

Malcolm X, whose real name was Malcolm Little, was born in 1925 in Omaha, Nebraska, and had a very unhappy childhood. When he was six years old, his father was murdered by members of the Ku Klux Klan. His mother suffered a nervous breakdown and her eight children were taken into care by the welfare department. At 21, Malcolm got into trouble with the police, was convicted of burglary and sentenced to prison. There he was introduced to the "Nation of Islam" or "Black Muslims". After his release in 1952, he changed his name to Malcolm X and became a leading personality of the Black Power Movement, which approved of violent actions against whites.

Malcolm X rejected Martin Luther King's peaceful tactics because he believed that racism should be opposed "by any means necessary" and consequently preached the violent way to solve America's race problem. He was convinced that the chasm between the races could never be bridged because all whites were evil and would never accept blacks on equal terms. The solution for the black man lay in racial separation, not integration. Therefore "the American black man should be focusing his every effort on building his own businesses, and decent homes for himself". Instead of counting on the white man's charity and generosity blacks should lean on their own strength and try to stand on their own feet. This alone could bring back pride and self-esteem. After 1964, Malcolm X softened his aggressive attitude and left the Black Muslims to form a rival group, the Organization for Afro-American Unity. In 1965, he was shot dead in New York by three assassins; all of them were Black Muslims.

Martin Luther King and Malcolm X in 1964

Thirty years after Malcolm X's death new radical black leaders raised their voices in protest and revived Malcolm X's doctrine of racial separatism. In 1995, Louis Farrakhan organized one of the biggest demonstrations in the history of the United States: "The Million Man March" of black American men on Washington. In his view the two groups, blacks and whites, were worlds apart and their different attitudes were irreconcilable. Therefore they should "get a divorce", which means they should live separately – perhaps one day even in separate states in the US. This view is not shared by the moderate black leaders in the NAACP (National Association for the Advancement of Colored People), still the US's largest black political organisation, which follows Martin Luther King's philosophy of reconciliation between the races.

Where Does the Civil Rights Movement Stand Today?

In 1957, federal troops were needed to guarantee the admission of nine black students to Little Rock Central High School, an all-white high school. Today that same school has about 2,500 students, the majority of whom being black. This fact illustrates the **achievements of the Civil Rights Movement** after decades of fighting for equality. On September 3, 1957, three years after the Supreme Court's landmark decision in the case Brown v. Board of Education to end the practise of "separate but equal" facilities, a group of nine black teenage students arrived to enrol at Little Rock Central High, but they were refused admission. President Eisenhower ordered soldiers to Little Rock, and on 25 September the students were allowed to enrol and Central High School was desegregated. Even then, however, President Eisenhower himself, who by his action had enforced the rights of **"The Little Rock Nine"**, said that legislation and government action alone could not bring about integration, because it could not change the people's hearts and overcome their suspicions and prejudices.

America did not become 'colour-blind', as Martin Luther King had hoped. More measures were needed to compensate for the injustices against blacks and other minorities. In 1961, for example, President Kennedy issued an executive order which obliged government contractors to "take affirmative action to ensure that applicants are employed and that employees are treated during employment without regard to their race, creed, color, or national origin". The Equal Employment Opportunity Act of 1972 which prohibited job discrimination for reasons of race, religion, colour, national origin and sex, encouraged a system of preferences to protect minorities and women from being discriminated against. The policy, which was called **"affirmative action"**, required employers, when they hired or contracted new staff, to prefer applicants from ethnic minority groups even if candidates from those groups had lower test scores than white applicants. The policy tries to help members of minority groups to compensate for disadvantages they had in relation to members of the white middle class. As many of them are confronted with problems on the labour market because they lack sufficient qualification or education, their acceptance rates at universities, for example, have been raised. In recent years, however, criticism of this system has increased. Whites complained of "reverse discrimination", and most people agreed that merit should be the only criterion for entry to a job and not race or sex. Even members of minority groups, who were supposed to profit from affirmative action, were not pleased about the preferential system. Black conservatives said their people became addicted to ethnic preferences instead of hard work. Following that criticism, affirmative action has been abolished in some states, but the US Supreme Court upheld the policy of racial preference on several occasions.

On January 20, 2009, **Barack Obama** was sworn in as the first African-American president of the United States. In his first inaugural address, he recognised the symbolic significance of his election, "[…] a man whose father less than 60 years ago might not have been served at a local restaurant can now stand before you to take a most sacred oath. So let us mark this day with remembrance, of who we are and how far we have traveled". In 2014, commemorating the signing of the Civil

Inauguration of Barack Obama, the first African-American US president, in January 2009

Rights Act of 1964, Barack Obama proclaimed: "Few achievements have defined our national identity as distinctly or as powerfully as the passage of the Civil Rights Act … As we reflect on the Civil Rights Act and the burst of progress that followed, we also acknowledge that our journey is not complete. Today, let us resolve to restore the promise of opportunity, defend our fellow Americans' sacred right to vote, seek equality in our schools and workplaces, and fight injustice wherever it exists. Let us remember that victory never comes easily, but with iron wills and common purpose, those who love their country can change it."

As Barack Obama pointed out, King's dream of harmonious and peaceful coexistence had not yet become reality. Today, the country is still struggling with issues of race. There are sociologists and observers who believe that racial divisions have even got worse. An indication of the **still existing racial divide** are the numerous confrontations between white policemen and African Americans which result in fatalities on both sides. Police shootings in which blacks were the victims, for example in Minnesota or Louisiana, erupted in violent protests of members of the black community, supported by the

Protests after the shooting of African-American Jamar Clark by the Minneapolis police in 2015

Black Lives Matter movement. There is statistical evidence that African American males are disproportionately more affected by police violence than males from other ethnic groups. On the other hand, when police officers are killed, as happened in Dallas and Baton Rouge, for example, the public outcry and fury is equally loud and nationwide.

Despite the progress made in the last few decades, Martin Luther King's optimistic vision still needs to be fighting for, or in Barack Obama's words: "The legacy of slavery and Jim Crow and discrimination didn't suddenly vanish with the passage of the Civil Rights Act or Voting Rights Act or the election of Barack Obama…We plant seeds…And somebody else maybe sits under the shade of the tree that we planted."

Education

Education in the Information Age

Parents, teachers and politicians alike agree that in our modern world today a good education is more necessary than ever. A country needs a qualified work force to compete in the global economy and the individual must be equipped to cope with the changes in today's world of work. Automation and technology have drastically reduced the proportion of unskilled jobs, while skilled jobs have increased. The rapid changes in science and technology mean that learning has turned into a lifelong activity and is no longer limited to the time spent at school. The Internet gives people direct access to a vast number of informational sources around the globe – the question is how to deal with this overwhelming amount of information, and with social media. Alarmed by the rise of social evils, such as drugs, violence and bullying in schools, educators demand a curriculum that touches more closely on contemporary social problems. They believe that character-building and social integration should take first place.

Anyone who takes part in the debate about reforming the educational system recognises the fundamental role which the public school system played in forming the American nation. It was education, supplied by schools and colleges, which integrated generations of immigrants into the nation and provided them with skills and knowledge to move upward within society. This function of education will become even more vital in the **multi-ethnic society** of today. The US classroom in primary and secondary schools is more diverse than at any time in the nation's history. To give an example, in 1972 6 per cent of students at American schools came from Hispanic families, by 1998 their number had increased to 15 per cent. In 2013, Hispanics made up 25 per cent of students at American elementary and secondary schools.

Decentralised School System

Some of the opportunities as well as many of the problems of education in the United States stem from the fact that the country's **public school system** is totally decentralised. There is no central federal agency or government department to control the whole system, nor is there a national curriculum. Although the United States Cabinet has a **Department of Education**, it has no authority over the operation of schools. The responsibility for education rests solely with the states in cooperation with local school districts. When the Founding Fathers drafted the Constitution they did not want to hand too much authority to a central federal government, and therefore reserved the right of individual states to control education. Consequently, when laws were passed making schooling compulsory – as early as 1642 when the Massachusetts Bay Colony passed such a law – responsibility for the schools was placed into the hands of **local school boards**. They each independently select the headmasters for their schools, the teachers and other personnel and decide on salaries. In order to provide funds for the newly founded schools the system of **property tax** was developed. This means that school boards raise money by taxing local homes or businesses at a certain rate. This system is still in operation today and leads to great inequalities, because the value of homes in different areas of a state varies greatly. When there are a lot of wealthy residents who can afford more expensive homes, the school board of this region will have more money available through property tax. This again means that these authorities can invest more in the schools they run, buying more computers and increasing teachers' salaries. On the whole, the funds raised by property tax are insufficient to cover school budgets, and this is where the federal government comes in. Although it has only an advisory function, today it provides more money for schools and school programmes than the local districts supply.

The K-12 System: From Kindergarten to High School
In the United States, as in most industrialised countries, schooling is compulsory. All American children are entitled to education at a public school, which means that the state has to provide schooling facilities. Students are also obliged to go to school for 12 years, during which time they receive elementary and secondary education. The term **K-12** is used to describe a student's 12 years of schooling, from elementary or primary education to the 12th form or grade. **Elementary education** starts in kindergarten and goes on to the 8th grade. It is followed by **secondary education**, at a secondary school or high school, which traditionally comprises grades nine to twelve. In the United States there are no separate educational systems like in Germany: there is one system only which is open to everyone. As in comprehensive schools ("Gesamt-/Gemeinschaftsschulen") students take different courses in the same buildings according to their talents and capabilities.

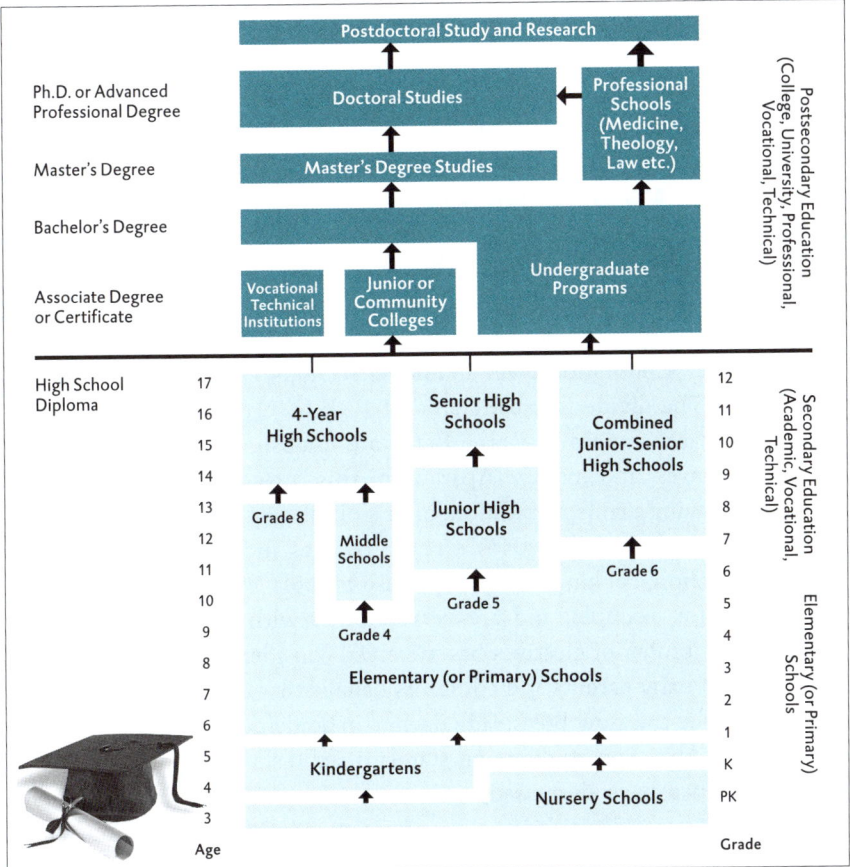

Although compulsory schooling usually begins when a child is 6 years old, most American children between the ages of 3 and 5 receive an earlier education. In the formative years before children reach school age, their drive for learning is met in **preschools** such as nursery schools, day schools or day cares and kindergartens. Kindergartens were introduced into the United States by German immigrants. Margarethe Schurz, wife of the German-born reformer and politician Carl Schurz, opened the first kindergarten in Wisconsin in 1856. Today kindergartens and day schools in America's cities and communities are normally run by churches or other institutions which are independent of local school systems.

Primary education begins when American children are 6 and start their first class or first grade. School days are from Monday to Friday, usually beginning between 7.30 am and 8.30 am, and lasting till 3 pm or 3.30 pm. Four basic subject areas are included in virtually all elementary schools in the United States: language arts (reading, writing, spelling, and related language skills), mathematics, science, and social science (usually history and geography). Physical education, music and art are also taught. The first aim is to teach "the three R's" – reading, writing, arithmetic. In spring 2000, the US Department of Education set as a goal for primary schools that every 8-year-old should be able to read.

Secondary education at high school comprises four years. It begins between grade 7 and 9 (depending on the state's regulations) and ends with graduation upon completion of the 12th grade or year. Some school districts divide secondary school into lower and upper sections, called junior and senior high school. The divide is usually around 10th or 11th grade. In most high schools the basic courses that are offered are English, science, mathematics, foreign languages, and history. Apart from this core curriculum, secondary schools, following a college tradition, offer a number of courses which are not required, the so-called "electives". These courses include performing arts, driver's education, cooking, and "shop" (use of tools, carpentry, and repair of machinery), for example, and are very popular with students. In the last 20 years the number of electives has increased considerably. This has pleased students, but many parents and educators believe that this practice is the primary reason for the slow but steady decline in academic standards. The average scores of American students on standardized tests of mathematics, reading, and science have decreased, and in international tests, such as PISA, American 15-year-olds perform average in science and reading, but lag behind in mathematics compared to other developed nations.

Some experts blame media consumption. Others argue that teachers are paid too little, with the result that good ones give up teaching, leaving it in the hands of less qualified staff who set their students easy tests so that all of them pass their exams and get a diploma. In spite of a general downward trend in performance, over 80 per cent of high school students complete school with an earned secondary diploma each year. The US education system does not conduct nationwide, official examinations at different levels as in Britain, for example. Nevertheless, students have to take a wide variety of tests at all educational levels to assess and evaluate their academic progress. Apart from examinations in class, there are also tests in laboratory work and supervised practical or field experiences. Homework, too, is evaluated on a regular basis. When students complete an academic term, they are given their marks, or grades, in each subject they studied as well as a final grade.

Higher Education (Post-school education)

About two-thirds of high school graduates continue in postsecondary education at colleges or universities, with the majority enrolling in bachelor's degree programmes. Regular colleges and universities are largely four-year institutions leading to a **B. A. (Bachelor of Arts)** or **B. S. (Bachelor of Science)**. Other high school leavers choose vocational training schemes which provide direct work-related programmes in skills such as secretarial training, auto mechanics, etc. or go to community or junior colleges – which offer **Associate Degrees** after two years. Since the 1960s it has become easier for students to start college or university because many of these institutions have modified their formerly rigorous admissions policies and also accept less gifted students. However, American politicians like to believe that in the United States education is the great equaliser moulding generations of adolescents into American citizens. The American ideal of equal opportunities for all looks different when you look beneath the surface. This is already evident when children start school. Children from upper-class or upper-middle-class families go to prep schools preparing their students for entry to the elite universities. But the disparities become even more obvious at **postsecondary level**. The great divider is the costs. Postsecondary education is not free – it is rather expensive, and is getting more so every year. Specially gifted students may qualify for grants or scholarships from public and private sources, but the majority have to pay for the cost themselves, e. g. by taking out a student loan. Consequently, when they graduate and start to work, American students are burdened by a considerable amount of debt for years to come. Obviously, students from wealthier families can go to better universities. The most prestigious and most expensive are in the north-eastern part of the USA and are referred to as the "Ivy League": Harvard (established: 1636), Yale (1701), the University of Pennsylvania (1740), Princeton (1746), Columbia University in New York City

Baker Library at Harvard University School of Business

(1754), Brown (1764), Dartmouth (1769), and Cornell (1865). Other American world class universities, for example, are Stanford (1891), The University of California, Berkely (1868), the California Institute of Technology (Caltech, 1891), and the Massachusetts Institute of Technology (MIT, 1861). All institutions of higher education compete with one another for research and foundation grants and public prestige. The reputation of some colleges and universities derives from their athletic programme and top sportsmen and -women they have enrolled.

A recent development in education is the growth in online and multimedia instruction ("e-learning") and "virtual schools". **E-learning** is the 21st century version of distance-learning through correspondence courses by mail, offering flexibility in the time, pace, and place of instruction – at home or in school. Teachers use the Internet to supplement regular classes or provide for special needs. Several state agencies, universities and local school districts run virtual schools that deliver courses primarily online.

US Schools

Schools in crisis

As early as 1955, the Hollywood film *Blackboard Jungle* shocked cinema goers because of its drastic scenes of violence in a New York City school. Numerous protests were raised against the screening of the film because it was feared that its showing would provoke even more violence. In the 1996 movie *Dangerous Minds*, starring Michelle Pfeiffer, a woman teacher of English struggled hard to teach a class of tough, frustrated and aggressive teenagers. There were no protests against the film, although little seemed to have changed at America's schools during the 40 years in between. Both films are based on the experiences of two teachers and mirror the concern of many Americans that education is in a crisis. The situation is especially desperate in inner-city areas where institutions lack money and staff to cope with increasingly hostile, rough and disinterested students.

The frequent **shootings** in American schools are the most shocking and disturbing symptoms that something has been going wrong with a part of young Americans in the last few decades. For example, in 1998, four girls and a teacher were shot to death and ten students wounded when two boys, 11 and 13, opened fire at their school in Jonesboro, Arkansas. One year later, at Columbine High School in Littleton, Colorado, two teenagers killed 12 of their fellow students and one teacher and injured many others. In 2012, a 20-

year-old first shot his own mother before opening fire at Sandy Hook Elementary School in Newtown, Connecticut, killing 20 children and 6 adults. It is not surprising then that schools have stepped up their security precautions to promote the safety of students, faculty and staff. It is common practice that visitors have to sign forms and get visitor's stickers, that students are not allowed out of their classroom without a pass, that staff members patrol buildings regularly, and that the whole school area is being surveyed by closed circuit television. All these precautions are necessary because of the easy availability of automatic guns in the country. Attempts to restrict the purchase of guns have so far been unsuccessful as they have been blocked by an influential rifle lobby.

For many years the high drop-out rate at American schools has been a serious concern of politicians and educators. There seems, however, to be a positive tendency: The dropout rate decreased from 12 per cent in 1990 to 6.5 per cent in 2014 as a result of a set of regulations enacted by former President George W. Bush. In 2001, Congress passed the **No Child Left Behind Act** (NCLB) which introduced fundamental changes in the curriculum of primary and secondary schools, with a special focus on minority students who tend to perform at lower levels than white students. The law required all states to carry out yearly tests in reading and mathematics at select grade levels in order to receive federal school funding. Teachers were also required to meet higher standards for certification. The NCLB was replaced by the **Every Student Succeeds Act** (ESSA), signed by President Obama in 2015. It abolished several of the most unpopular provisions of NCLB and gave states more flexibility in determining how and when the standardised federal tests would be given. States were also permitted to include other measures of student and school performance.

School Desegregation and Racial Integration

In 1954, the **Supreme Court** took one of the most important decisions in the history of the United States concerning racial relations. The court's ruling put an end to the "separate but equal"-doctrine that had been established since 1886 in the case Plessy v. Ferguson. The "separate but equal" policy permitted racial separation of public facilities including schools. In the South, and in other parts of the country as well, black students were especially disadvantaged not enjoying the same chances as white students because the authorities spent much less money on schools for blacks than on schools for whites. In 1950, the father of a black child took the education authorities of Kansas, Texas, to court because he wanted to achieve equal opportunities for

Busing programs were introduced to promote integration of black and white students at school.

all children. Other families also appealed to the court, and after hearing a series of school-segregation cases, the Supreme Court finally decided unanimously in 1954 that segregation was against the Constitution. The court overthrew the ruling of 1886, concluding "that in the field of public education the doctrine of 'separate but equal' has no place. Separate educational facilities are inherently unequal." The opinion spurred the **Civil Rights Movement** and brought about fundamental changes in race relations across America. Following the court's ruling to desegregate schools the government immediately adopted the policy of "**busing**" to promote racial integration. Children from black families were taken by bus from disadvantaged urban areas to schools in predominantly white areas – and vice versa, white children were bussed into black neighbourhoods. This measure of forced integration was never popular and after widespread opposition from whites and, to a lesser extent blacks as well, the policy was eventually abandoned. Many sociologists believe that the problem of racial integration today is even more complex and difficult to solve than in the 1960s and early 1970s. Then the problem of racial segregation was a problem which still concerned mainly two ethnic groups, blacks and whites. Today the issues of diversity are much more complicated due to the dramatic growth in the Latino and the Asian-American population. Half of the recent population growth in the US has been in just three states – in Florida, Texas and California. The majority of the growth in those areas, and in school enrolments particularly, is Latino. People from Latin American countries settle mainly in the Southern and Western states of the USA and form their own communities. Living together they retain their culture and traditions by keeping their own language. In some parts of Miami and Los Angeles tourists can make themselves understood today if they speak Spanish.

Bilingual Education

Almost 5 per cent of Americans speak English less than "very well" and many do not speak English at home. There is also an increasing number of Hispanic-Americans who speak "Spanglish", a mixture of English and Spanish with few rules and many variations. In their conversations speakers use the word that comes first to mind – be it Spanish or English. Linguists call this mix of two languages "code-mixing". Some Hispanics use this new type of language because they find it too difficult to switch over to English completely, others want to keep their Latin American heritage.

In order to reach their Hispanic voters during election campaigns, Republican and Democratic candidates have some of their political commercials broadcast in Spanish. During his presidency, Bill Clinton had a wide range of government documents translated into Spanish so that Latinos could read and understand vital government information on education and health – particularly on immunisation, adoption and parenthood. In 1974, a Supreme Court ruling ordered schools to provide extra help to pupils whose English was deficient. Following this decision, states with high immigration rates introduced the system of "Bilingual Education". In California – home of half the nation's immigrants – and a number of other states bilingual education became compulsory. Students who were considered "proficient of limited English" were taught both in English and in their mother tongue. It was hoped that by using this method integration could be facilitated. However, the bilingual approach met with increased criticism. Because of the high immigration numbers, anti-immigrant sentiment in the United States grew and campaigns to make English the nation's official language gathered strength. A lobby group called "US English" expressed fears that the American ideal of the melting pot would come to an end and campaigned for English as the only language of instruction in schools. The general feeling was that English should be used as a unifying force to achieve assimilation. Therefore, in 1998, Californians voted for the adoption of an amendment known as Proposition 227, which demanded replacing the bilingual programmes with "English immersion" classes where immigrants would "either swim or sink", as one teacher put it. In 2009, the US Supreme Court stated that SEI (Structured English Immersion) was significantly more effective than bilingual education. However, in the course of time, views changed and in 2016 Proposition 227 was repealed, which means that languages other than English can now be used again in public educational instruction.

The Search for Alternatives: Private Schools and Home Schooling

Many parents, teachers and politicians complain about the low academic standard at American schools. Politicians of both parties, Republicans and Democrats, have made numerous efforts to raise student achievement and improve school standards, for example by advocating the establishment of nationwide tests. Months after becoming president in 1989, Republican George Bush called a meeting of the nation's 50 governors, all of whom agreed in a declaration that it was necessary to improve the quality of education. During Democrat Bill Clinton's presidency the US Congress passed the **Goals 2000: Educate America Act** – a legislation which gave states government aid to help them devise their own academic standards. However, due to the decentralised organisation of the US education system the federal government cannot enforce a change. Many schools adopt the recommendations of the Department of Education and tighten their requirements, others do not or cannot. In poor neighbourhoods, where school boards can only draw on rather limited funds to equip their institutions, the situation is getting worse. Incidents of violence, drug dealing, overcrowding and under-qualified teachers make parents look for a way out of the dilemma to find better ways of educating and qualifying their children. They make use of the fact that although school attendance is compulsory in the United States it need not be at a public school. The alternatives parents have found are **home schooling** and **private** or **charter schools**.

Whereas public schools do not charge for tuition, parents who send their children to private schools or have decided on home schooling have to bear the tuition cost themselves. Despite this disadvantage, about 3 per cent of all school children today are tutored at home, and about 10 per cent are enrolled in private schools. Private schools run by religious groups are called **parochial schools**. The largest systems are operated by the Roman Catholic and Lutheran denominations, and there is also a great number of Jewish schools. Within parochial school education, the most rapid expansion is within the Muslim community. Other private schools and colleges are sponsored by individuals, by foundations or firms. A recent development within the American system of education are the so-called **"charter schools"**. Charter schools use public funds, but they are run with more freedom and flexibility than typical public schools. The US government, Congress and a number of states such as Michigan and Arizona support this type of school, hoping that students' performance will be much better than in public schools. Furthermore, it is believed that the funding of the charter school system will do away with the long-standing inequality between schools in cities and in the country, caused by **property tax funding**. As to the teaching, supporters say charter schools allow innovative teachers to try new ideas, especially because these institutions are free to create their own curriculum and tend to be small. On the other hand, critics argue that running and funding these schools is a waste of money which the public school system could use better and more effectively. They add that there is little evidence that charter schools improve student achievement in the long run. To support students from "low income families", for example, a number of states have introduced the system of school vouchers. Parents receive money to pay for some or all of their child's tuition at a private school or a public school in another district. The voucher programme has been criticised for being ineffective and too expensive, and for draining much-needed resources from public schools.

An increasing number of families are taking the education of their children into their own hands. The movement which is becoming more popular is called **"home schooling"** and means that school-aged children are being taught by their parents at home. Home schooling replaces full-time attendance at a school, but some children enrol part time at a campus-based school or share instruction with other families. The reasons why parents turn their backs on the public education system are manifold. Some are worried about the low academic standards at the schools in their area and are convinced that their children will profit from intensive home schooling. Religious belief is also an important factor. Other parents do not want to send their children to overcrowded "factory schools", which they regard as unable to deal with both learning-disabled and highly gifted children. Others put high emphasis on teaching moral and ethical behaviour, which, in their view, is neglected at public schools. As far as college admission and graduation is concerned, homeschooled students do as well as other students or even better.

Religion

The United States – a Religious Society

America can be described as one of the most religious societies in the world. There is a great variety of different denominations, and several hundred thousand churches, temples and mosques all over the USA prove the remarkable religious vitality of the American society. It should be noted that figures about membership are often supplied by the churches and they may therefore vary because the United States government does not collect religious data in its census.

- American **Protestant** churches (ca. 46.5 %) spread across more than 200 particular denominations including, for example, Baptists, Methodists, Lutherans, Anglicans and Episcopalians (who combine Protestant and Roman Catholic traditions), and Quakers.
- Roman **Catholics** are the second largest denomination with some 69 million adherents (ca. 20.8 %). Due to Hispanic immigration the number of Catholics is increasing.
- About 1.9 % of Americans are of **Jewish faith** (defining themselves as being religious, or primarily culturally or ethnically Jewish).
- An estimated 0.9 % of the US population are **Muslims**; because of the immigration from Islamic countries it is the most rapidly growing religion in the United States.
- **Hinduism** and a number of other faiths have risen as a result of immigration from India and other countries.
- Almost 25 % of Americans are **non-religious**.

Many Americans express their faith openly. They wear T-shirts that promote religion ("Jesus saves"), or talk frankly about their convictions. Religion also seems to have turned into a commodity on the market. There is a growing world of religious rock music; religious radio and television broadcasting have become a major element of American religious life. Whereas in most other western societies the number of church-goers is on the decline, in the United States six people in ten say that religion plays an important part in their lives.

Separation of Church and State

The first settlers emigrated to the New World primarily because they were looking for a place to practise their faith without being persecuted by the government. Consequently, to avoid any interference from the government in religious matters the authors of the Constitution of the United States saw to it that there was a strict separation between state and church. England served as a warning example which they did not want to follow. The British Sovereign was "Defender of the Faith" and Supreme Governor of the Anglican Church, the state church. This close link was established in 1534 when King Henry VIII had separated the English Church from Rome in order to obtain a divorce from his first wife Catherine of Aragon. He had then proclaimed himself "Supreme Head of the Church of England", thus starting a tradition alive until today. When the American colonists drew up their Constitution at the end of the 18th century they had two aims in mind – as far as religion was concerned. First of all, they wished to protect the right of each individual to **free exercise of religion**. The right of free religious worship was not extended to the Native Americans, whose religious practices and traditions were treated with little respect by the white invaders. In the second place the creators of the Constitution wanted to prohibit the establishment of religion through the state. Therefore, the **First Amendment** to the US Constitution reads like this: "Congress shall make no law respecting an establishment of religion, or prohibiting the free exercise thereof …". The two most influential politicians advocating this double principle were Thomas Jefferson and James Madison. Jefferson had gained fame and respect as the author of the Statutes of Religious Liberty for Virginia, in which he presented himself as a fervent defender of religious freedom. Together with his co-author James Madison, who held similar views on freedom of worship: "The Religion then of every man must be left to the conviction and conscience of every man; and it is the right of every man to exercise it as these may dictate. This right is in its nature an unalienable right." Both men were responsible for the wording of **Article VI of the American Constitution** which reflects their conviction: "No religious test shall ever be required as a qualification to any office or public trust under the United States." By accepting this principle the representatives at the Constitutional Convention in Philadelphia broke with European tradition and opened public office in the federal government to people of all faiths or none at all. The separation of church and state keeps the government out of religious matters, but it has also practical consequences. The congregations do not receive any financial support from the government, and there are no taxes deducted from people's income as in Germany. Many advocates of the full separation of church and state argue that this system makes the churches more alive because they are forced to find their own resources in contrast to state-supported churches.

Debate about the First Amendment

Although the First Amendment aims at a separation between church and state there are numerous examples that in practice there has often been a **connection between politics and religion**. From the early days of the colonists to the present day, religions and religious beliefs have played a significant role in the political life of the United States. During the American War of Independence religion offered a guarantee to the average American that the revolution against the mother country was justified in the sight of God. Later, when the

white settlers moved into Indian territory, and displaced and killed the Native Americans they did this in the "name of God". The newly developed concept of **"Manifest Destiny"** reassured them that it was the godly mission of the white man to conquer the wilderness and civilise "primitive savages".

In his song "With God On Our Side", for example, singer and poet Bob Dylan criticised the self-righteousness of many Americans in

Allegorical depiction of the concept of "Manifest Destiny". Painting by John Gast (1872)

believing that all their wars had been fought for a just cause and that the American people had always had "God on their side". Every session of the US Congress begins regularly with a prayer by a minister. When addressing the American public via television every president ends his Message on the State of the Union with the word "God bless you" or "God bless America". At the inauguration ceremony the new president is sworn in and confirms the oath he takes with the formula "So help me God". These practices are only a formality or a tradition, but there are also religious issues which have caused social conflict and strife.

The **controversy over the First Amendment** arises from the fact that it has been interpreted in two different ways. Some people see it as the Founding Fathers' provision that the government should stay out of religion completely. The opponents of this view argue that the First Amendment must not be used to make America a religion-free country. A vivid illustration of the difficulty to determine how far government influence can be allowed is the long-lasting debate over **prayers** before school sports matches. When, for example, the school authorities in Santa Fe allowed students in June 2000 to initiate and lead prayers over the public-address system before the football games a parent group opposed this permission and filed a lawsuit arguing that the school district's policy violated the First Amendment by creating a "pervasive religious atmosphere". The argument over public prayer has been put before the US Supreme Court more than once. Of major importance for the current debate is a decision taken in 1992. The court ruled 5-4 that school-sponsored prayers at graduation and other official school functions violated the First Amendment. The court reaffirmed that the Constitution guarantees that the government cannot coerce anyone to support or participate in religion or its exercise. However, these rulings have made the opposition even stronger in their efforts to campaign against a policy which in their opinion is hostile to religion. Religion, they say, is too important to America's history and heritage to keep it out of the country's schools. It may never be possible to resolve the apparent inconsistencies of the First Amendment; even scholars of the Constitution find it hard to draw a clear line between state interference and religious freedom. The compromise could be that religious practices at schools cannot be demanded, but on the other hand, must not be denied.

Religious Diversity

There was another reason for Jefferson and Madison to insist on including the separation of church and state into the Constitution. Not all the Founding Fathers believed in the same God, or in any God at all come to that. The Declaration of Independence refers to a deity, but only in the most general terms – "Nature's God", the "Creator", "Providence". These words were chosen in order not to offend the doubters and deists (who believed that God had designed the universe, then left it to nature to run). Jefferson was a renowned doubter, urging his nephew to "question with boldness even the existence of a God".

There was also a practical reason for the framers of the Constitution and the Bill of Rights to **support religious pluralism**. In the 18th century many immigrants arrived in the New World because they wanted to be free from government interference in the practice of their religious beliefs. The politicians assembled in Philadelphia realised that it was practically impossible – and politically unwise – to establish one religion for the emerging new nation, because none of the different religious groups was strong enough to dominate the others. This means that the religious diversity, which we observe in the United States today, has its roots in the **history of immigration to the New World**. Through the centuries, the religious landscape of America has expanded greatly.

Religious Groups

Protestants

The first settlers who came to North America were Puritans and Calvinists who were looking for a place where they could practise their faith without being persecuted by the government. These groups had developed in the wake of the Reformation in the 16th century. Because of the Protestant tendency of their religious belief the Separatist Puritans were regarded as outsiders, as non-conformists, by the established state church, the Church of England, and were not allowed to practise their religion freely. The dissenters left England and first moved to Holland where they found temporary asylum. They formed the Separatist congregation at Leiden, but eventually left the Old World because they had obtained permission by the Virginia Company to settle in America, and set sail across the Atlantic. The **Puritans**, who were later known as **Pilgrim Fathers**, hired the ship Mayflower and left England in September 1620. The historic voyage took 65 days, during which two of the 102 passengers died. In November 1620 the colonists dropped anchor at what was later to become Provincetown (Massachusetts). Still on board of the ship, 41 men signed the so-called **Mayflower Compact**, which became the basis of government in the Plymouth Colony, and elected John Carver their first governor.

Stamp from 1970, commemorating the 350th anniversary of the Landing of the Pilgrims

In the 18th century America became a religious refuge for many Protestant communities which eventually gave the new American nation a mainly Protestant face. Today Protestantism is still the dominant creed. After the arrival of the Pilgrims, more and more followers of different religious groups arrived in the North American colonies. Anglicans settled in the South, and Puritans in New England. Although the majority of the sects had come in flight from religious persecution in their homelands, they did not show the tolerance they themselves had searched for towards other religious refugees. People with diverging theological views were not always accepted by the original Pilgrims and consequently established new colonies of their own in which they enjoyed religious liberty. New England became the home of various Puritan groups, Pennsylvania and New York had substantial numbers of Lutherans, minor German Protestant groups, and members of the Society of Friends or Quakers. Early Virginia was largely identified with Baptists and Methodists. However, in the course of time, the religious groups became more tolerant and began to learn to live together. The Constitution eventually contributed to settling and avoiding sectarian conflicts by guaranteeing religious freedom for all Americans.

Very soon different schools within the Protestant movement developed. On the one hand, there were the liberal Protestants who were reading and interpreting the Bible in a new way. They questioned the validity of biblical miracles, traditional beliefs about the authorship of biblical books and sought a lessening of doctrine. Today this branch is referred to as "mainstream Protestantism". On the other hand, there were – and still are – the conservatives, often called "evangelicals" because of their enthusiasm for the gospels of the New Testament. They believed that departures from the exact truth of the Bible were unjustified. The largest Protestant groups include the Baptists, Methodists, Lutherans, and the Presbyterians.

Baptists

The Baptist Church first appeared in England and Wales in the early 17th century. The first Baptist church in the New World was established in 1638, at Providence, Rhode Island, by Roger Williams, an English colonist who refused to associate himself with the Anglican Puritans. The name of the community derives from its most noted practice of **baptism of adults** by immersion. Baptists believe that only adults are prepared to make a personal confession of faith in Jesus Christ. In Baptist church services the emphasis lies on Bible reading and preaching. Baptists strongly believe in the Bible and interpret the scripture literally.

In the late 18th and 19th centuries the Baptist church found an increasing number of followers in the USA, especially among the Southern black population. Black Baptist churches, and their ministers, played an important role in the civil rights movement of the 1960s, led by Martin Luther King. In 1998, a statement of delegates of the strong and influential Southern Baptist Convention received wide media coverage. In their resolution on the family the Baptists delegates included their belief that a wife should "submit herself graciously" to her husband. Whereas most media criticised the statement, it was welcomed by church members who wanted their church to give them and the society as a whole stronger moral guidelines.

Methodists

The largest single group of Methodists is the United Methodist Church with about 7.6 million members in the United States. The Methodist movement was started in England by John and Charles Wesley, and George Whitefield in the 18th-century who organised small "societies" within the Church of England for Bible study, prayer, and preaching. The **Wesleyan Movement**, as it was first called, soon spread worldwide because the Wesley brothers and their associate Whitefield travelled widely, preaching to large and enthusiastic crowds of working people. After John Wesley's death in 1791 the Methodists separated from the Church of England, and in the 1840s the Wesleyan Methodist Church of America was founded. The group played a major role in the fight against slavery. Three large black Methodist churches were also organised in protest against racial prejudice.

Catholics

The number of Roman Catholics in the USA increased in the 19th century when hundreds of thousands of Irish people were driven from their homeland by the **Great Famine**. Potato crop failures in Ireland had forced them to leave their homes, so that by the time of the Civil War (1861–1865) over one million Irish Catholics had come to the United States. As they were not usually welcomed by the Protestant majority the Catholics started their own schools in which the teaching of Catholic doctrines and morality was given great priority. Because of their discipline and quality of education these private schools eventually attracted a growing number of non-Catholic students. Until today they have retained their prestige and are still popular places of instruction, although they do not receive public funds and are financed by tuition fees paid by parents. In recent years, Catholic parents sought financial assistance from the state for maintaining their separate educational system, reasoning that they saved the government money by sending their children to private schools. However, the Supreme Court ruled that if the state supported religious schools this would violate the First Amendment. Governmental subsidies were therefore unconstitutional.

Prejudices against Catholics have had a long tradition in the United States. **Anti-Catholic feelings** were so deep-rooted that they could still be observed more than a hundred years after the first waves of immigration of Irish and Italian Catholics. In 1960, some Americans opposed the presidential candidate of the Democratic Party, John F. Kennedy, because he was a Catholic, arguing, if elected, Kennedy would receive his orders from the Pope in Rome. In spite of these absurd accusations Kennedy won the presidency, but he has remained the only Catholic American president to date. In 2009, Joe Biden became the first Catholic vice-president of the USA.

In the US today, the Catholic Church is the denomination which is one of the most diverse regarding ethnic and cultural background. Due to immigration from Latin America, and above all from Mexico, Hispanics are the fastest growing group and now account for 38 per cent of Catholics.

Jews

Similarly to Catholics, Jews were a small minority in the first years of the American republic. Most Jews first came from central Europe and belonged to the Reform movement, a **liberal** branch of Judaism which had modified the old doctrines and adjusted to modern life. Therefore they were readily accepted into society when they first arrived in the United States and anti-Semitism was not a big problem before the Civil War. However, the situation changed and anti-Semitism developed when the immigration waves of the 19th century brought an ever larger number of **orthodox** Jews from Russia and Poland to the United States. These newcomers who strictly observed the traditions (dress, celebrations) and laws (e. g. dietary laws) of Judaism and preferred to live closely together in certain quarters of the cities were often regarded as outsiders.

Ultra-orthodox Jews in Brooklyn, New York

Today more Jews live in the United States than in any other country, including Israel. Many came between 1935 and 1945 from Germany to escape from Nazi persecution, but since 1950 most Jews have come from the Middle East and Eastern European countries. Not all of them kept to the traditional rites and practices, but adopted a non-religious and more liberal position. Intermarriages between Christians and Jews further promoted integration. Jewish citizens have made important contributions in all walks of American life, especially in the fields of politics, finance and banking, art, the press, science and in the entertainment industry. Famous Jewish Americans are or were, for example, writer Arthur Miller, composer George Gershwin, or actress Natalie Portman. Many Jewish immigrants moved rapidly into the professions and universities, where they became intellectual leaders. Famous Nobel laureates were, for example, Albert Einstein, Milton Friedman, Henry Kissinger, and Bob Dylan.

Islam

Immigration to the United States in the 19th and 20th centuries changed the mix of religious groups considerably, but America's overall heritage remained primarily European. This situation changed in the mid-1960s with the revision of the immigration laws, when more non-European immigrants were admitted. New groups from Asia and the Middle East brought their cultural and religious values and contributed significantly to the growth of the Islamic faith. Membership numbers for the Muslim community in the United States are hard to come by and can only be estimated (about 3.3 million). It is now the ethnically most diverse religious denomination in the USA.

Seeking an alternative to their "slave identities", many African Americans converted to Islam as they believed that many of the original slaves would likely have been Muslim. As outward proof of their new identity they adopted Muslim names, the most famous example being boxer Cassius Marcellus Clay, who after joining the Black Muslims gave up his "slave name" and assumed the name Muhammad Ali. He also refused to be drafted to the US army arguing that he was a Black Muslim minister and therefore a conscientious objector.

In the aftermath of September 11, 2001, attitudes toward Muslims and Islam changed drastically. Hostility against Muslims surged again after major terrorist attacks in Europe (Paris, Brussels, Nice) and the US (Boston, San Bernardino, Orlando). In the face of terrorist attacks and hate crimes, many Americans question the willingness of Muslims to adopt Western values, whereas the great majority within the Muslim community itself identifies with the US and is equally concerned about Islamist extremism.

Mormons

America has been a fertile ground for new religions. The Mormon and Christian Science Churches are the best-known of the faiths that have their origins in America. About 6.5 million people in the United States are members of the Mormons or Latter-day Saints. The church was founded by Joseph Smith in 1830. He claimed having had visions of God in which he was told to establish the restored Christian church. The Angel Moroni, one of the heavenly messengers, Smith maintained, directed him to some golden plates, inscribed in a hieroglyphic language, which he translated. His translation is the **Book of Mormon**, which describes the history, wars, and religious beliefs of a group of people who migrated from Jerusalem to America – long before Christopher Columbus discovered America. Smith attracted a small group of followers who moved to northern Missouri and then to Illinois. The Mormons met with opposition and were persecuted because Smith had introduced polygamy into Mormonism. In 1844, an armed mob assassinated Smith, and Brigham Young became his successor. In 1846, Young organised and directed a march from Illinois across the plains and mountains to the Great Salt Basin in Utah. After Congress had passed anti-bigamy laws (1862 and 1882) and the Supreme Court had ruled that religious freedom did not allow the practice of polygamy, the Mormons discarded plural marriage. One of the main aims of the church is missionary work. The Mormons have no professional clergy; therefore all members are encouraged to perform religious service. Young men and women devote two years of their lives to working as missionaries. The abstention from tea, coffee, alcohol, and tobacco is laid down in a code of health, called "Word of Wisdom". Mormons oppose the Equal Rights Amendment because in their view the equality of the sexes upsets family life.

Christian Science

Christian Science was founded by Mary Baker Eddy in 1879 as the **Church of Jesus Christ**, Scientist. The central belief is that God is the only reality, and the material world, with all its suffering, strife, and death, is unreal. It is considered to be a misunderstanding or deformed view of the divine universe. Illnesses are also regarded as delusions of the human mind and consequently can be healed by praying for the right understanding. Members of the church refuse medical or other material means to cure diseases and rely on divine law in times of sickness. Christian Science parents who claim the right to withhold medical treatment from their children have been convicted of criminal negligence. Mary Eddy formulated the rules of the group in the Manual of the Mother Church (1895). The rules say that Sunday services are to consist mainly of readings from the Bible and the textbook of Christian Science, which was also written by Mary Baker Eddy. The church has no ordained clergy, and readers, both men and women, are elected from the membership to perform the services. The highly respected **Christian Science Monitor** is a general weekly newspaper published by the Christian Science Publishing Society, but it carries little about the doctrines of the Christian Science church.

Other Churches

The religious landscape in the United States is so very diverse due to the extraordinary tolerance American society has always shown towards people of different beliefs and convictions. "Live and let live" has been the motto since the republic was first founded and thus the US has provided a home for many small sects from overseas. In the 18th century a conservative Protestant group, the Mennonites, fled from persecution in Europe and settled in Pennsylvania. People called them Amish after their Swiss bishop Jakob Amman. The members of the Amish communities live simple lives, wear plain clothes and reject the usage of modern machinery and technology. The Hollywood film *Witness* with Harrison Ford made the group known worldwide and

every year thousands of tourists visit the Amish communities in Pennsylvania and neighbouring states. Other churches with a significant membership are Jehovah's Witnesses, the Seventh-Day Adventists and the Disciples of Christ. In 1954, L. Ron Hubbard founded Scientology, recognised as a church in the USA but not in Germany because of its totalitarian measures of mind control and the fact that members are forced to contribute large sums of money.

Traditional Amish buggy

Sects and Cults

The great tolerance in religious matters has given rise to a number of groups with extremist or esoteric beliefs, many of which tend to glorify a founding figure, like for example Bhagwan Rajneesh in Oregon in the 1970s. Other sects are the Unification Church, also called Moonies, known for their mass weddings, and the Hare Krishnas. Most Americans regard these cults as rather bizarre, but as long as their members abide by the law they are free to exercise their "religion". On the other hand, the eccentric leaders of those cults often have had a detrimental influence on their followers. In 1969, Charles Manson, who thought of himself as Christ, ordered members of his cult to commit nine cold-blooded ritual murders. One of the persons killed was the pregnant wife of the film director Roman Polanski. A mass suicide of 900 brainwashed followers of a religious commune occurred in 1978. A massacre took place at a farm owned by the **Branch Davidian** religious sect near Waco in Texas in 1993. For 50 days, agents of the FBI and the Bureau of Alcohol, Tobacco and Firearms laid siege on the sect's heavily fortified compound because they wanted to arrest cult leader David Koresh on weapons charges. In the end 86 people were shot or burned to death and the farm was destroyed completely. Great parts of the press and the public later criticised the FBI, arguing that an inflammable form of teargas had been used in the assault. The Department of Justice, however, defended the actions of the agents.

Religious Movements and their Impact on Society

The Great Awakening

America has seen several religious revival movements which cut across denominational lines. Inspired by their evangelical fervour revivalists travelled across the continent with their message of salvation through Christ alone, evoking a deeply personal and emotional response in thousands of Americans. In the middle of the 18th and at the beginning of the 19th century two waves swept through the states: the **First** and the **Second Great Awakening**. The most fervent preachers of this evangelist movement were the **Methodists** and **Baptists**. Around 1740, several Protestant denominations united in an effort to revive interest in religion. They had noticed that in the American colonies people had developed a sense of self-righteousness which had caused them to neglect their search of God and religious practices. The most famous preacher who sought to inspire the communities with new enthusiasm was the English travelling preacher George Whitefield, who became the leader of **Calvinistic Methodism**. Whitefield stressed the importance of vital religious experience as the cornerstone of effective religious life. However, more conservative parsons did not welcome the confusion brought about by the Great Awakening, arguing that emotions destroyed man's rational control of his destiny. A revival of the movement, called the Second Great Awakening, occurred in the early 19th century with the same purpose of revitalising the churches spiritually. New organisations were formed, such as the American Bible Society and the American Sunday School Union, to carry God's word into the outlying parts of the expanding new nation. Missionaries travelled into the West to encourage the settlers to read the Bible, build churches, attend Sunday church services in order to advance morality and political stability – and to convert the Native Americans.

Evangelists and the Electronic Church

Like their forerunners, the evangelists of today lay great emphasis on the believer's personal relationship with Jesus Christ and his or her commitment to the demands of the New Testament. In their preaching they call on the hearer to confess his sin and believe in Christ's forgiveness. They aim at promoting the reading of the Bible and try to convert people to Christian belief. Instead of travelling the country, like the 19th century revivalists, the preachers of today make use of radio, television and the Internet. This is why they are called "preachers of the Electronic Church".

The most prominent US evangelist of the 20th century and head of an enormous organisation devoted to the spread of the Bible was **Billy Graham**, who, to a large extent, followed the footsteps of the 19th century revivalists. Graham gained a worldwide reputation for his charismatic preaching and evangelistic crusades. He was not interested in complicated theological concepts and did not hesitate to use methods of modern publicity, from organising promotional material to leading a "Motorcade for Christ". The Billy Graham Evangelistic Association was founded in 1950 to promote crusades, develop radio and television programmes and produce films. He met important politicians, monarchs and hundreds of celebrities, and served some American presidents as advisor.

Lakewood Church in Houston, Texas, is a "megachurch" whose services are broadcast weekly on several TV channels.

The Rise of the Christian Right

Observers from Europe are always fascinated and sometimes puzzled in which way the revival movement has always used modern means of communication to spread the word of God. The new rise of the Christian Right began in the late 1960s and 1970s – when conservative Christians saw American principles undermined by permissiveness and decadence. The conservative and often fundamentalist TV evangelists demand a literal belief in the words of the Bible, believing that Jesus Christ will once again reign on earth. In their moral crusades they speak out against contraception, abortion, homosexuality, same-sex marriage, embryonic stem cell research, pornography and immoral behaviour in general. The Internet has helped the Christian Right to popularise the movement's stances on cultural and political issues, as well as to recruit members and sell merchandise. Observers criticise these commercial activities as well as the star cult surrounding TV preachers, several of whom have turned spreading the gospel into a profitable business.

Religious Lobbying
The political significance of the Electronic Church lies in the fact that it strengthens the religious right in the United States. Its most fervent supporters are to be found in the so-called **"Bible Belt"** in the South and Midwest of the US. In early 2000, for example, conservative religious groups put pressure on TV stations to ban the screening of a cartoon series in which God was portrayed as an amiable character, wearing dark sun glasses and a green T-shirt. Protesters in deeply religious areas attacked the animation show as "tasteless and trivial". TV stations in Utah, Idaho, Missouri, Indiana and Louisiana were the first to cancel the programme.

The teaching of Charles Darwin's **theory of evolution** at public schools is also contested in US states with a strong religious movement. In his famous book *On the Origin of Species by Means of Natural Selection* (1859) Darwin argued that all forms of life on Earth developed from common ancestors. Over billions of years, life gradually evolved into the incredible variety of forms and species that exist today, including human beings. Fundamentalist Christian groups reject this theory as anti-religious because it conflicts with the biblical story that God created the world and all forms of life. This belief, known as **creationism**, is widespread, while the younger generations increasingly accept the theory of evolution.

Some people observe the activities of the radical religious groups with suspicion and are worried about their increasing influence. In the 1980s, groups of the Christian Right began drumming up support for conservative candidates in elections. Because he promised to support the establishment of school prayer and anti-abortion legislation Republican Ronald Reagan secured the support of conservative voters in the Bible Belt to achieve electoral victories in the 1980 and 1984 presidential elections. Although members of the Religious Right lobbied politicians massively and tried to put pressure on them to make laws and legislation less liberal, in reality their efforts had little effect. Once elected, US politicians have hardly ever given in to religious lobbying. When Bill Clinton, a Baptist, ran for the presidency in 1992 he made it clear that he was a firm believer and often used religious metaphors in his public speeches. The hopes, which the Religious Right had put in him, were disappointed, because Clinton introduced liberal legislation regarding homosexuality and abortion. From then on, many conservative evangelicals and fundamentalists viewed him with suspicion and deep-seated antipathy. In 1998, when Clinton vetoed a bill which was intended to ban late–term abortion, he was heavily criticised by leaders of several religious groups including his own denomination, the Southern Baptist Convention. However, Clinton stood by his decision and was even supported by 36 religious leaders in the Religious Coalition for Reproductive Choice.

These examples show that the American people watch developments in the field of religion with open eyes. The vivid discussions and controversies are ample proof that the Constitutional separation of church and state which was laid down in the First Amendment has made religion stronger and not weaker. Religion is a more vigorous institution in the United States than in almost any other country where state and church are closely linked.

Media

The Press

The Freedom of the Press

Serious journalism is an **important cornerstone in any democracy**. It is no wonder that in authoritarian regimes the media are kept under strict control and the freedom of the press is suppressed. Thomas Jefferson, one of the Founding Fathers of the United States, even went so far as to write: "If it were left to me to decide whether we should have a government without a free press or a free press without a government, I would prefer the latter." Jefferson and his political friends believed that it was the fundamental right of citizens to be informed about all sides of an issue without governmental interference. This conviction of the importance of the freedom of the press is laid down in the First Amendment to the Constitution of the United States: "Congress shall make no law respecting an establishment of religion, or prohibiting the free exercise thereof; or abridging the freedom of speech, or of the press; or the right of the people peaceably to assemble, and to petition the government for a redress of grievances". These words are the basis for America's tradition of a free press.

History of the Press in the USA

The founders of the United States thought it essential to stress the importance of an uncensored press in order to distinguish their new government from that of Britain. They remembered only too well what had happened to the first newspaper published in the American colonies. The paper *Publick Occurrences Both Forreign and Domestick* was launched in 1690 in Boston, Massachusetts, but was forced to close down by the colonial government after just one issue. It took fourteen years before John Campbell was allowed to print the first regularly published colonial newspaper, *The Boston News-Letter*. The British continued to censor the press and prosecuted persons who dared to criticise the British Crown. To comply with the strict regulations, American editors avoided controversy and restricted the contents of their papers to local news and social events. With the passing of the **Stamp Act** (1765) the British levied a direct tax on all papers required for official business in the American colonies. This tax was also put on newspapers in order to make them more expensive and thus reduce their circulation. Although the Stamp Act was repealed in 1766 it increased the resistance of the colonists against their English masters – a resistance which eventually culminated in the American War of Independence. In 1776, the editors of the colonial papers printed the **Declaration of Independence** on the front pages to demonstrate their support of the revolutionary movement. In the 19th century, millions of immigrants arrived in the United States and the number of people who wanted to read a newspaper to learn about the American way of life increased rapidly. As new printing presses were invented and the railways made rapid transport across the country possible, more and cheaper papers could be printed and distributed. Newspaper publishing and advertising became a profitable business, and the number of American newspaper titles more than doubled between 1880 and 1900. In 1846, six New York newspapers formed the first news agency to be run by the newspapers themselves, the New York Associated Press, which today is known as **Associated Press (AP)**. Another important American news service, **United Press International (UPI)**, was created in 1958.

One of the most prestigious daily papers in the USA and the world today is **The New York Times**, founded in 1851. Adolph S. Ochs (1858–1935) acquired the paper in 1896 when it was making a loss, and built it into a most re-

The New York Times Building in Manhattan

spected and reliable news source. The NYT's motto, "All the News That's Fit to Print", is the compact version of its mission: to provide detailed and objective coverage of events. The publication of the Pentagon Papers in 1971 was an impressive example of the paper's investigative journalism and its function as political watchdog and defender of a free press. For its outstanding achievement in journalism, the NYT was awarded the Pulitzer Prize more often than any other news organisation. One of New York's most frequently visited landmarks, Times Square, owes its name to the once nearby building of the New York Times newspaper.

Another influential newspaper publisher was **Joseph Pulitzer** (1847–1911), who helped establish the pattern of the modern newspaper. In 1883, he bought the failing *New York World* and increased its circulation by making the paper both informative (reports about political corruption) and entertaining (comics, sports coverage, women's fashion coverage, and illustrations). In his will, Pulitzer provided for establishing the Columbia School of Journalism and the **Pulitzer Prize**, which has been awarded annually since 1917 for outstanding public service and achievement in American journalism, letters, and music. Pulitzer's opponent was **William Randolph Hearst** (1863–1951). With his sensationalist style publications he soon earned enough money to start a number of other profitable papers and magazines which grew into an empire comprising major newspapers, telegraphic news facilities, radio stations, and news and motion picture syndicates. In 1941, Orson Welles used the life of media magnate Hearst as the model of Charles Foster Kane, the main character in his film *Citizen Kane*. Hearst unsuccessfully tried to suppress the film which is generally considered one of the greatest American movies ever made. **Hearst Media** is one of the biggest media companies in the US today.

In 1923, Henry Luce and Briton Hadden started their weekly **news magazine** *Time* which reported on political events, cultural activities, sports, movies, personalities, and specific social issues. The success of *Time* prompted other companies to start similar magazines, for example *Newsweek* in 1933. Both are still the best known news magazines in the US, and they became the models of the German equivalent *Der Spiegel*, which began publication in 1947. Henry Luce was also the founder of another news magazine which he called *Life*, in 1936. *Life* was different in as much as its emphasis was on pictures, not the written word. The German journalist Henri Nannen created *Stern* in 1948 using *Life* as model.

Today, most Americans still get their information about current events mostly from television. Consequently, since the arrival of this medium in the 1950s readership of newspapers has steadily declined. Many publishers ran into economic difficulties and eventually ceased publication of their papers. Many newspapers saw their only chance of survival in printing regional and local news which would not be covered by the TV news programmes and news channels. This is why American readers can choose from a large number of regional papers, but the US national press does not offer the same variety as the British, for example. The pressure of rising production costs, including higher wages for the workers, and poor management drove many dailies out of business. Many editors and publishers saw the only way to survive in combining forces with others. This marked the beginning of the big newspaper chains. The largest newspaper chain is the **Gannett Company**, whose flagship newspaper, *USA Today*, is one of the largest-selling daily newspapers in the country. The Gannett Company owns some 90 newspapers with an overall circulation of more than 7 million.

From the 1950s to 1990s, it was television which presented a threat to the existence of newspapers, today it is the **Internet**. Most papers have online versions, and some offer their content free of charge, because their pages carry advertisements to finance the enterprise. More recently, however, the number of media which charge for access to Internet content has risen. *The Wall Street Journal*, the *New York Times* and nearly all Gannett publications, for example, introduced a **paywall**, which means only users with a paid subscription can read articles and features. Free email newsletters and other online services have further contributed to the decline in newspaper subscriptions and circulation rates. Although some media experts predict that within the next decades printed newspapers will be replaced entirely by electronic information services, others maintain that the printed word will never disappear and remain an important part of our modern information society.

The Role of a Free Press

The press is regarded as the fourth authority in a democratic state – the other three are the legislative, executive and judicial powers. It informs the public on important events and, to a certain extent, exercises control on the government and local administration. Parts of the printed press and, more recently, an increasing number of Internet communities or non-profit organisations (e.g. WikiLeaks) have appointed themselves the role of watchdogs over morals and decent behaviour.

Two examples from US history stand out as triumphs of **investigative journalism** and illustrate the vital role a free press plays in the control of the government. Reporters and journalists of two of the most respected papers in the United States, *The Washington Post* and the *New York Times*, informed the public about events which the governments of the day would have liked to conceal. The two spectacular investigations and publications of the journalists became known worldwide as the **Watergate Scandal** and the **Pentagon Papers Affair**. In 1971, the *New York Times* obtained a copy of a top-secret document which outlined the history of America's war in Vietnam. The classified document, called the Pentagon Papers, had been prepared by the Department of Defense. In June 1971, the *New York Times* published excerpts from the secret study, which suggested that the government had misled the

American people about the war. The government took the paper to court, claiming that the publication of the information violated the Espionage Law and caused "irreparable injury to the defense interests of the United States". The Supreme Court ruled that the publication of the papers could continue and thus upheld the right of the press to perform its function as a check on official power. During the presidential campaign of 1972 five burglars led by a former CIA (Central Intelligence Agency) employee broke into a hotel and office complex, the Watergate, in Washington, where the Democratic Party had its headquarters. They were working for the Republican Party's Committee to Re-Elect the President, then Richard M. Nixon (in office 1969–1974). With extraordinary persistence and accuracy two *Washington Post* reporters, Carl Bernstein and Bob Woodward, traced the connections of the burglars to the White House. They revealed that high officials who were very close to President Nixon were involved in the planning and the execution of the burglary. At first Nixon and his aides denied any involvement in the Watergate break-in, but with their investigations the reporters finally proved that Nixon him-

self was aware of illegal measures to cover up the affair. When Nixon realised that he was likely to be impeached, he resigned. For their coverage of the political scandal that led to the first resignation of a president in US history, Bernstein and Woodward won the 1973 Pulitzer Prize for public service. In 1974, they wrote the best-seller *All the President's Men*, which was made into a successful film.

Carl Bernstein (left) and Bob Woodward

Journalists and the press also played an important role in the revelation and publication of illegal operations of the American National Security Agency (NSA). In 2013, former Central Intelligence Agency (CIA) employee **Edward Snowden** handed classified documents to the media to make the world aware of the intricate spying methods applied by the NSA, revealing the huge scale of the NSA's global surveillance programmes, which also affected friendly governments.

In 2015, a whistleblower, who used the pseudonym "John Doe", leaked a set of more than 11 million confidential documents to investigative journalists to expose illegal methods of tax evasion and corruption. The German newspaper *Süddeutsche Zeitung* first agreed to look through the documents. This happened with the aid of the International Consortium of Investigative Journalists (ICIJ), among them also US journalists. The documents were termed **"Panama Papers"** because a law firm from Panama had helped wealthy individuals, among them many politicians, business tycoons and celebrities, to establish more than 200,000 offshore letterbox companies with the aim of hiding money from public scrutiny. In 2016, after the documents had been thoroughly analysed for a year, the first news about the papers were made public in over 100 newspapers, TV stations and online media in 76 countries, among them the United States.

Television

Today the most important networks are the "Big Three" – **NBC** (National Broadcasting Company), **CBS** (Columbia Broadcasting System) and **ABC** (American Broadcasting Company) – plus the Fox Broadcasting Company and CW Television Network. The "big three" news channels are Cable News Network (CNN), Fox News Channel, and MSNBC.

Most TV stations in the US are commercial stations financed by advertising revenue, which means the TV companies sell time for advertisements which are broadcast in breaks during programmes. A non-commercial station is **PBS** (Public Broadcasting Service). TV advertising is expensive and firms spend enormous sums to advertise during a special event such as the **Super Bowl** because the programme is watched by millions of viewers. As soon as a programme or a show loses its popularity it is taken off the air. Special organisations (e. g. Nielsen Media Research) establish the ratings of the programmes and inform TV producers and advertisers. To attract as many viewers as possible, programming is concentrated on entertainment and diversion. Popular shows include **situation comedies** (such as *Big Bang Theory, Modern Family, New Girl* and *Two and a Half Men*) and comedy-variety shows. There are all sorts of TV series featuring detectives, investigators, special agents, lawyers, and the police. In the last few years, among the shows with the highest ratings have been *NCIS* (Naval Criminal Investigative Service), *Criminal Minds, CSI* (Crime Scene Investigation), *Person of Interest* and the medical drama *Grey's Anatomy*. An increasingly popular genre of so-called reality television are talent shows such as *American Idol, America's Got Talent* and *The X Factor* in which amateur singers, dancers, magicians, comedians, and other performers of all ages compete against each other.

Soap operas, which were first produced for radio and daytime television, enjoy continued support. The name derives from the fact that the first sponsors of such shows were soap manufacturers. In 1978, CBS screened the first weekly soap at prime-time (after 8 o'clock in the evening), *Dallas*. Its success led to the creation of many similar shows. Quiz and game shows also enjoy a consistent popularity, as do **talk shows**. Famous talk show hosts are Johnny Carson (1925–2005), Oprah Winfrey, David Letterman, Jimmy Kimmel, Jon Stewart, and Larry King. King alias Lawrence Harvey Zeiger, was probably the most renowned interviewer in the world. For more than 20 years his show *Larry King Live* on CNN was watched in millions of households around the world. Over the years, he interviewed almost all of the prominent people in the world – from Mikhail Gorbachev to Frank Sinatra and Yasser Arafat, from the Dalai Lama to Bill Clinton. Although heavily criticized because its participants used to do less talking and more fighting, *The Jerry Springer Show* became one of the top-rated talk shows, surpassing long-time talk queen Oprah Winfrey.

The increase in the number of subscribers to cable television networks (such as HBO) and **on-demand Internet** streaming services (such as Netflix) is a great challenge to the big three TV companies NBC, CBS and ABC. Cable networks or streaming services attract viewers because they are renowned for producing high-quality series (such as *The Sopranos, The Walking Dead, Breaking Bad, House of Cards,* or *Game of Thrones*). Many people also prefer to watch media on their smartphones and other mobile devices whenever they please. Cable and wireless providers like AT&T invest in or are in the process of acquiring media and entertainment companies, for example Time Warner, thus combining distribution and content and making profits in both business fields.

The Media and Elections

Before the arrival of the Internet, Americans mostly relied on cable and television news programmes as their primary sources of information about government, current events and elections. Since 2008, when Barack Obama first won the presidential race, the importance of the **Internet** at election times has increased tremendously. E-mails and social media tools such as tweets and facebook posts are used to inform a large audience in no time. Campaigners use the Internet to raise funds, organise action groups, muster volunteers and mobilise voters. Candidates use social media as a cheap and effective method to reach a large part of the electorate, especially the younger voters.

In spite of the Internet, **television** has retained its importance to influence a mass audience. During campaigns for the Senate or presidential elections extensive advertising crusades are launched to win the support of the undecided voters. If the contestants and their campaign managers agree to present views in a series of live presidential **TV debates**, precise rules, including the places, times and topics, are laid down. Hundreds of analysts and consultants in the election committees start work to prepare their nominee for his/her appearance on screen. Media experts say, the visual impact of the electronic medium is so great that viewers pay more attention to how the speakers look, what facial ex-

TV debate between Hillary Clinton and Donald Trump during the 2016 presidential election campaign

pressions and gestures they make than to what they actually say. To describe this fact, Marshall McLuhan (1911–1980) coined the phrase "the medium is the message". In 1960 the first presidential TV debate was held, and helped decide the presidential race between John F. Kennedy and Richard Nixon. Nixon had charged his opponent that he was too young and too inexperienced to serve as president. However, in the disputes Kennedy made a much better impression on the audience and the debates turned the tables. Kennedy won the elections in November 1960 and became the nation's first real "television president" who used the new medium for his political aims. For the first time, he allowed live broadcasts of news conferences to convey his policies of the "New Frontier" to the American people. Since then clever strategies have been developed to make politics understandable and attractive for the average viewer. At election times, in particular, politics is "made for television", which means it is simplified and reduced for the TV news. Long debates and detailed discussions have disappeared. Today, election campaigns in European countries have become very much as those in the United States. Party and election managers in Britain, France and Germany hired the know-how of the men and women behind the successful presidential campaigns in the US. Tony Blair first used these "spin doctors" in the 1997 General Election in the United Kingdom.

During the 2016 presidential election campaign the allegiances of the two major news channels, Fox and CNN, became more than evident. Fox News is the more conservative station and supported Donald Trump's candidacy for the White House, while the more liberal CNN was in favour of Democrat Hillary Clinton. Fox News is owned by a company of media mogul Rupert Murdoch. His media company has frequently been subject to criticism because of its aggressive, sensationalist reporting style and the use of unethical means of obtaining information. CNN, launched in 1980 and part of Time Warner, enjoys a better reputation, but has also been subject to allegations of **biased reporting**. Fox News repeatedly criticised the policies of President Barack Obama, especially his Health Care Reform, and devoted significantly more time than competitor CNN to airing live coverage of Republican presidential nominee Donald Trump's campaign rallies, live events, and press conferences.

The Internet and Social Media

Social network sites have experienced an enormous growth in recent years and logging on to these sites has become daily routine for millions of people. Users can stay in touch, exchange messages about private or work-related affairs, post views on topic issues, send photos or consume videos, films, or music. The most important social media companies, for example Facebook and Twitter, were started in the United States and have their headquarters in California.

In his novel *The Accidental Billionaires* the American author Ben Mezrich gives a vivid account of the founding of **Facebook**, the world's most popular social networking, site by Mark Zuckerberg, while he was still at Harvard University in 2004. Facebook offered shares to the public in 2012 and acquired the photo sharing service Instagram and the cross-platform messaging service WhatsApp. **Google** was started as a search engine in 1998, but has since extended its digital services and products enormously. In 2006, for example, the company bought the video-sharing website YouTube. In his dystopian novel *The Circle* (2013), Dave Eggers explores the disturbing scenario of an increasingly powerful Internet company which is about to control society and people's private lives in a totalitarian way.

Social networks may be free of cost, but they **collect data** and information about the activities of their users, such as the sites they visited, the searches they executed etc. In this way, Facebook, Google, Twitter, Instagram, and other sites know a great deal about the relationships, interests, and spending habits of their members and make efficient and profitable use of the data collected. As access to the social networking sites is free of charge, the companies earn most of their money from online advertisers and publishers. For example, marketers, retailers, advertisers, and publishers pay for using Doubleclick, owned by Google, which helps "to turn searchers into customers" (Doubleclick slogan), which means delivering adverts tailored to users' preferences. The technology allows the display of adverts on websites or control of how often and for how long an ad is shown to a browser. The fact that social networking sites track users and collect data has been criticised as constant surveillance and an invasion of users' rights to privacy.

What is also criticised when it comes to the widespread use of social media is the so-called "**social media bubble**", in which one's own opinions and preferences are mirrored and reinforced by mathematical algorithms so that users are rarely, or not at all, presented with divergent points of view or alternative ideas. Another severe problem on social media sites is the proliferation of sexist, racist or homophobic hate posts or of outright lies, which rapidly spread throughout the net. As a lot of people get news and information mostly from social media posts, the impact of these services can have a profound effect on real life, as could be seen in the 2016 presidential election, which was not dominated by the exchange of arguments and facts but often by claims based on dubious sources.

Economy

Today the United States still has the world's most powerful economy, with China being its fiercest competitor. In 2007 and 2008, the USA experienced a **financial crisis** triggered by a crisis in the housing market caused by risky loans – especially mortgages – made to borrowers with poor credit histories. Panic spread through the stock markets and the banking sector in the USA and then to all over the world as financial institutions had bought many of these dangerously speculative loans and debts, and investment banks had gambled without restraint. In order not to lose more money, banks reduced credits and loans sharply, which made investments or expansion for healthy companies more difficult or even impossible. An economic downturn set in which represented a major challenge for governments all over the world, costing the taxpayers millions to stabilise banks, and the financial market. Since then the US economy has been recovering, but without much gain for the lower and middle classes.

Until the early 20th century, European countries, above all Great Britain, were the world leaders in economy. That leadership was lost to the United States for several reasons. First of all, the American government did not interfere with people's economic activities, there were hardly any business regulations or limitations. What is more, the country had **generous tax laws** which made it easy and profitable for private individuals or investors to set up firms and businesses. The **liberal regulations** and the prospect of relatively quick success attracted millions of immigrants. America was the land of opportunities, free from class barriers and privileges based on heredity, so that people could concentrate on business. Another factor which explains the rise of the US economy is the fact that American firms profited from an ever-growing **consumer market**. Due to immigration the American population increased tremendously and consequently the number of prospective customers.

Agriculture

Agricultural Belts
The natural environmental conditions which are necessary for farming – such as soil, climate, and topography – determine the crops produced, the techniques employed and the type of farm organisation. The especially advantaged

Huge wheat field in a Midwest state

areas for farming in the USA are the so-called agricultural belts, vast stretches of land which follow climatic zones. The **Dairy Belt** extends through the green pastures of New England and the Great Lakes area and provides milk products. The climate in the Dairy Belt area is rather moist, the growing season is short and the thin glacial soil less suited to arable farming. The **Corn (Maize) Belt**, sometimes referred to as the "bread basket of the world", runs through the Midwestern United States from the Allegheny Mountains to Missouri and occupies the country's largest continuous body of fertile level land. Farming in this region produces cheap, good-quality maize, beef and many other sorts of farm produce. The **Wheat Belt** in the Great Plains west of the Mississippi is one of the world's chief granaries. More than once, US farmers helped nations confronted with a hunger crisis to overcome their problems by supplying them with wheat grown in abundance in the Wheat Belt. Spring wheat grows west of Lake Superior and the prairie provinces of Canada, winter wheat is produced from northern Texas to Missouri. The **Cotton Belt** extends through the south of the eastern USA from North Carolina to Texas. Because of inefficient farming methods and monoculture the soil in the Cotton Belt was often exhausted in the past. As a consequence, many farmers and farm workers had to leave their land and migrate to the industrial North to find work in the factories there. Today, more up-to-date farming methods are applied. **Fertilisation** and **rotation** with other crops like peanuts have helped to revitalise the soil.

The Ups and Downs of US Agriculture

The basis of the formidable success of the US economy was laid in a sector which has changed dramatically over the last 200 years: in agriculture. At the time of the War of Independence (1775–1783) the Americans were a nation of farmers: over 90 per cent of the population was engaged in agriculture. Peasants and smallholders left their European homelands in great numbers because most of the land was in the hands of the landed gentry. The prospect of changing from tenant to land owner made millions leave for the New World where conditions for agriculture were ideal in most parts of the country. Land was abundant, but there were not enough people to work on it. The farms were mainly run by individual farmers and their families, and were scattered over enormous areas of land. These family farms became the basis of North American agriculture, and their owners developed a strong sense of individualism and self-reliance.

Throughout the 19th century new tools and equipment were invented and new techniques introduced. Machines were taking over the work of haying, threshing, mowing, cultivating, and planting. The mechanical reaper *(Erntemaschine)* changed the production methods on American farms. Apart from making life easier for the farmers these new inventions also helped to boost the agricultural output considerably. Productivity was further pushed by the arrival of more settlers. The **Homestead Act** of 1862 promoted westward migration across the Mississippi River by maintaining the existing pattern of small family farms by offering a "homestead" of 160 acres to each family of settlers for a nominal fee. In the end the government had achieved more than it had intended, because farms produced more than that which was needed and after the Civil War overproduction became a serious problem. As a result, prices fell and farmers received less for their products. However, things improved, in particular because the federal government had created the Department of Agriculture in 1862 which took a direct role in agricultural affairs.

In the 1920s and 1930s, American farmers again experienced desperate decades. The average income per head in the USA in 1929 was $750, the average farmer's income was less than half, because farmers had become victims of their own success. During the years of the **First World War** farmers had increased production to sell food to Europe. They had cultivated new land, taken on new machinery. When the war was over, farmers in the USA were producing more than they could sell. As a consequence prices for agricultural products fell dramatically. It was not worth taking crops to the market, because freight costs were higher than the prices farmers could

Homeless family walking on the highway bound to California during the Great Depression of the 1930s

President Franklin Delano Roosevelt
(1933–1945)

achieve for their produce. Tens of thousands of farmers could not meet their mortgage repayments and were driven into bankruptcy. In his novel *The Grapes of Wrath* (1939; Pulitzer Prize, 1940) John Steinbeck tells the dramatic and emotionally gripping story of a family from impoverished Oklahoma, a state which was affected by severe drought during the economic depression of the 1930s. The Joads are a family of sharecroppers who leave their farm, and come to the promised land of California, where they become the lowest of the migratory farm labourers. With his **New Deal** Action Programme of 1933 President Franklin Delano Roosevelt saved many farmers and their families. After his election to the presidency in 1932 he promised to restore the confidence of the American people and to bring America out of the **Great Depression**. Roosevelt stated in his first inaugural address that "we have nothing to fear but fear itself". In several radio talks, the so-called "fireside chats", he addressed the American people, explaining the legislation of his administration. In his second chat he presented a plan to relieve the plight of the American farmers.

A newly created government agency, the Agricultural Adjustment Administration (AAA), set fixed quotas for most agricultural products to avoid overproduction and thus keep the price of farm produce up. Pigs were slaughtered, the cotton crop was ploughed into the ground, and farmers were paid not to cultivate some land. Parts of Roosevelt's rescue plans have been incorporated into today's farm policies of the federal government in Washington that promotes up-to-date farming techniques. The depression of the 1930s has also made farmers change from monoculture to a greater diversity in farming, because it makes them less vulnerable to climatic hazards and crises in the world market.

From Family Farms to Agribusiness

The small immigrant farmer who used to work on his land to provide for himself and his family has disappeared almost completely. Today large corporations own the land and use modern machinery to improve the agricultural output. Manual labour has been reduced, draught animals have been replaced by machines. Farming has been lifted from the self-survival level to a commercial level. It has become big business and therefore been given a new name: **agribusiness**. The agribusiness sector is much larger than the traditional farming industry. It is not only concerned with the production, purchasing and marketing of foods, it also fabricates and sells fertilisers, insecticides, and supplies machinery and equipment. The development of improved techniques in the areas of irrigation, soil analysis, fertilisation, plant and animal breeding and the application of advanced managerial methods have raised productivity enormously. Today less than 2 per cent of the US population work on farms, but they produce more than can be consumed in the country. About one-third of the cropland in the United States produces crops destined for export.

Chemical Farming and Genetically Modified Crops

The production methods in US agriculture have exacted their price. Above all, conservationists criticise that American farmers have damaged the environment because they use large amounts of artificial fertilisers and chemicals to kill weeds and pests. The modern farmer has been taught by agricultural experts that the best way to increase output is to use **chemical fertiliser** and then protect the harvest from insects with generous applications of pesticides. It is not surprising then that toxic chemicals used in agriculture have found their way into the nation's water, food and air. Even more worrying is the fact that the giant poultry, hog and cattle factories do not merely produce meat, but also a horrendous crop of drug-resistant germs. The problem is the overdosing of farm animals with **antibiotics** to kill bacteria in the animals. About half of the antibiotics produced in the United States are being used in animals – and most of these are used not only to fight animal diseases, but to stimulate quick growth. Scientists are concerned that the strongest germs might mutate and become completely resistant to antibiotics. Because of the negative effects of chemical farming more and more Americans are buying organic produce despite the higher prices, and in the last few years, the number of **organic farms** in the US has increased rapidly.

"**Genetically modified (GM) crops**" are made by inserting genetic material from one species of plant, bacteria, virus, animal or fish into another species. The idea is that these new plants are resistant to pests so that farmers would have to use less toxic chemicals, and can produce healthier food. Still there are many unsolved questions. Critics argue that we simply do not know the long-term consequences for human health and the wider environment when we release modified plants into nature. They warn we might cause "genetic pollution", because genetically engineered crop plants are capable of transferring their genetic qualities to wild plants. This transfer might eventually create "super-weeds" which could disrupt the biodiversity of an area. People's reservations are also based on the fact that we do not yet have adequate laws and regulations for the application of biotechnology in foods. As the US is the world's leading producer of GM crops, and the biotechnology industry is an important part of the American economy, the US is less restrictive to the development and application of GM organisms in food. However, many American consumers support the labelling of modified foods. Finally, in 2016, a law was enacted which regulates labelling of GM food nationwide.

Industry

19th century: Industrial Expansion and Economic Rise

The Industrial Revolution started in Britain in the middle of the 18th century. It was a revolution which changed production methods and also transformed the country from a rural to a predominantly urban society. **Industrialisation** in the United States differed in several ways. It did not bring about a radical change of society, as there was no European-style society characterised by the gap between aristocratic rich and labouring poor, to change. American industrialisation was not based on the invention of new tools and machines – Americans adopted and improved innovations already used in Europe. Finally, the growth of American industry happened at the same time as the growth of the American nation and could therefore be better planned. The waves of immigration increased the country's population and provided a steady stream of workers who contributed to the expansion of business and industry.

In colonial times, the British used their North American colonies as suppliers of raw materials and consumers of colonial goods, which were produced in Britain. So the British could sell the manufactured products at much higher prices than they had paid for the raw materials. Farming and trading were therefore the main businesses in the United States until the early 1800s when in the course of the Napoleonic Wars (1803–1815) British goods were hard to obtain and the United States had to produce most of its own goods, with the textile industry in New England becoming the first important industrial sector. The **Civil War** and the **building of the railroads** further spurred industrialisation in the young United States. The war between North and South claimed the lives of tens of thousands of people and devastated the economy in the South, but it nevertheless stimulated industrial development, mainly in the Northeast. Uniforms, shoes and, above all, weapons were needed to outfit the large number of soldiers. A new method was developed to produce firearms by designing a gun of identical parts and machinery which allowed unskilled workers to put the parts together. US manufacturers adopted his system in other sectors of industry, thus making mass production possible. The second great stimulus came from the construction of the railroads which began in the

Completion of the First Transcontinental Railroad in 1869

1830s. The pace of building accelerated after 1862 when Congress set aside public land for the first transcontinental railroad, generating a great demand for coal, iron, and steel. Railroads became increasingly important to the expanding nation as goods and heavy loads such as coal, iron ore and minerals could be transported fast and efficiently. The railroads linked out-lying areas of the country into the world's first transcontinental market and pioneers could spread their settlements into hitherto unconquered territories. Industrialisation had progressed to such an extent that by the end of the 19th century the output of America's factories exceeded the output of its farms. On the international level, Britain had lost its place as leading industrial country to Germany and the United States – two countries which had started industrialisation later, but with newer and more advanced machinery.

20th Century: The World's No. 1 Industrial Power

Whereas the economies of Germany and other European countries were badly damaged due to the devastations of two world wars the US economy profited from the war effort in Europe and managed to become the greatest productive country in the world.

Until 1917 the US stayed out of the First World War and did well selling weapons, ammunition and food to the allies, the profits being invested in new industries. Using innovative production methods such as the **assembly line**, manufacturers after World War I could produce **consumer goods** – cars, radios, vacuum cleaners – faster and more cheaply. Lower costs also meant lower prices for consumers and higher wages for the workers. Thus more and more Americans were able to afford products which for a long time had been regarded as luxury items, revolutionising the American way of life in the 1920s. The car, chemical and film industries experienced unprecedented booms which were supported by the advertising industry's methods (radio commercials, posters, commercial travellers) to persuade people to buy the new products.

However, large sections of society, in particular farmers, blacks and the unemployed, did not as much share in the country's prosperity. When eventually even more people lost their jobs and so did not have the money to buy consumer goods the US economy faced a serious crisis, the most spectacular sign of which was the **Wall Street crash in October 1929**, when hundreds of thousands of Americans, who had invested in the stock market, lost their savings. This collapse of the US stock market marked the beginning of the **Great Depression**. During his campaign for the presidency in 1932 Franklin D. Roosevelt promised a **"New Deal"** for the country to help "the forgotten man", the farmer who had lost his land or the worker who had lost his job. After his election Roosevelt introduced new laws to restore people's confidence in the banking system, to create jobs for the masses of unemployed and help the impoverished farmers. Although some laws were invalidated by the Supreme Court, Roosevelt set up the **Second New Deal**, which helped the US economy to recover. However, it was the military-industrial production in the Second World War which finally brought an end to economic depression.

After 1945, the USA experienced a **post war economic boom** which brought about an expansion of the middle class. However, from the 1970s onwards, some economic branches faced serious challenges. The car industry, for example had to fight competition from other countries, above all Japan. On the other hand, new sectors developed and boomed. Manufacturers of airplanes, cellular phones, microchips and space satellites, microwave ovens and high-speed computers netted high profits. One of the reasons for the success of the manufacturing industries was the high degree of automation, which meant fewer workers were needed than in traditional industries and production costs were cut, making the goods cheaper but hundreds of thousands of workers jobless. Today one sector is gaining more and more importance: the service industry, which includes banking, insurance and finance services, entertainment and recreation, hotels and restaurants, communications, education and office administration. With the loss of so many industrial jobs, America seems to be changing into a "post-industrial" society.

The American Idea of Free Enterprise

Since the days of the Founding Fathers and the pioneers Americans have placed high value on the idea of individual liberty and self-reliance. This concept is also reflected in the American approach to economic matters: Everybody should be able to decide in which business to operate and be allowed to pursue profit freely – which above all meant without restraint from government intervention. The consequences of economic freedom and the function of market forces were explained by the economist and philosopher Adam Smith in his publication *An Inquiry into the Nature and Causes of the Wealth of Nations* (1776), the first major work of political economy. The economic doctrine advocating that commerce and trade should be permitted to operate free of controls of any kind was referred to as "laissez-faire" (which means "leave alone to do") and became the corner stone of capitalism and has been the driving force behind the American economy. Americans still rely very much on private enterprise and initiative, although over the years more government regulation has been introduced into the economic system. A look at the lives and works of three American entrepreneurs serves as an illustration of the typically American economic spirit, which created the American Dream, the vision of the dishwasher who makes it to become a millionaire.

John Davison Rockefeller

J. D. Rockefeller (1839–1937) was the guiding force behind the creation and development of the Standard Oil Company, which grew to dominate the oil industry and became one of the first big trusts in the United States. He became a legend in his own lifetime and a rather controversial figure, because for some he remained the supreme American success story, for others he was the symbol of unrestrained capitalism. J. D. Rockefeller was born as the second of six children. The family lived in modest circumstances. School was difficult for him and after only two years of high school he went to work in Cleveland, Ohio, in 1855 as a bookkeeper for a small food firm. In 1859, together with his partner Maurice B. Clark, he formed Clark & Rockefeller, a food firm handling grain, hay, meat and other goods. Like many other businesses, their company prospered during the Civil War. As he was deeply religious, he began to give 10 per cent of his earnings to churches. In 1863, Rockefeller gave up the meat and grain firm and entered the oil business by setting up a refinery in Cleveland. In 1870, he founded the Standard Oil Company of Ohio, which soon grew into a complex organisation dominating almost every aspect of the oil business: the piping, refining, and marketing of American petroleum. In order to keep control of this industrial giant, Rockefeller formed the Standard Oil

Trust in 1882. The trust was soon regarded as a monopoly whose practices endangered free competition, and the government eventually decided to take action. In 1890, Congress passed the **Sherman Act**, the first of three antitrust laws. With this law the government wanted to ensure that market competition was not threatened by an organization or cartel with a monopoly on a given product. The other two major federal antitrust laws are the Clayton Act and the Federal Trade Commission Act of 1914. The federal lawsuit against Standard Oil ended in 1892 with the court demanding the dissolution of the trust. Rockefeller dissolved the Standard Oil Trust and transferred control to companies in different states, but he maintained control through Standard Oil New Jersey. In 1911, the Supreme Court forced the separation of the 38 companies which Standard Oil controlled into individual firms. By this time Rockefeller had retired from active leadership in the company and become more engaged in his philanthropic activities. He gave away some $ 550 million of his fortune and, in 1913, founded the Rockefeller Foundation.

Henry Ford

Henry Ford was the American industrialist who further developed the technique for the production of firearms, introducing the moving **assembly line**. Ford was born in 1863 near Dearborn, Michigan. At the age of 17 he took a job in the Michigan Car Works and began building engines and motors in his spare time. In 1903, he and his partners founded **Ford Motor Company** and started selling a few cars. Ford's vision was to build a car for the masses: an inexpensive, highly dependable, easy-to-repair car. Ford used all his early profits to design this car, and in 1908 presented his **Model T**, nicknamed "Tin Lizzie", which he offered for $ 825, about half the price of many other cars of the day. With Ford's Model T the era of **mass production** began. The increasing demand for the T made Ford devise the ideal way to manufacture it. He and

Ford assembly line in 1913

his team introduced the modern assembly line, a method in which conveyor belts brought car parts to workers. When the system was first introduced, the amount of time required to build a Model T could be reduced from 12.5 hours to 93 minutes, with cars coming off the line in three-minute intervals. The car's retail price temporarily dropped to $260. When the last Model T car left the factory in 1927, more than 15 million "Tin Lizzies" had been built. Industrial managers studied Ford's manufacturing techniques in order to break down work processes and design more efficient and less costly ways of organising tasks. Ford's innovation was also criticised, however, because work on the assembly line can be monotonous, and has a numbing effect on workers – and bored, depressed workers tend to do inferior work. Charlie Chaplin satirised the new production method in his film *Modern Times* (1936). In today's car factories, robots have taken over the tiring routine jobs. Ford did not only revolutionise production methods, he was also an innovator in labour policy. He introduced the minimum wage, the 8-hour-day and the 40-hour week.

Labour and Management

American workers never developed the same class consciousness as workers in England, for example; the belief in the American Dream – that everyone can make it – was strong for a long time. In spite of this, however, also workers in the US united to fight for their rights. The first major effort to organise workers' groups on a nationwide basis appeared with The Noble Order of the Knights of Labor in 1869 whose place in the labour movement was gradually taken over by the American Federation of Labor (AFL), which was founded in 1886 and was only open to skilled workers. During the great industrial growth between 1865 and 1900, the work force expanded enormously, especially in the heavy industries, and strikes, sometimes accompanied by violence, became commonplace. The first violent conflict between employers and workers occurred with the **Great Rail Strike of 1877**, when rail workers across the nation went out on strike in response to the third pay cut in a year. The most militant union was the International Workers of the World (IWW), which was founded in 1905. The IWW openly called for class warfare and demanded the overthrow of capitalism through strikes, boycotts, and sabotage. The IWW opposed the participation of the United States in World War I and called for work stoppages in the midst of the war. The federal government took legal action against IWW union leaders and by 1925 the union had disappeared. In 1935, a new union mainly for industrial workers was formed, the Congress of Industrial Organizations (CIO). The organization grew rapidly; by the late 1930s it had more members than the AFL, the union for skilled workers. AFL and the CIO merged in 1955 to form the AFL/CIO. Union membership, however, has declined since the early 1980s due to anti-union legislation crafted during the Reagan administration (1981–1989), and de-regulation of numerous industries. In addition, industries which were union strongholds, such as the heavy industries, are on the decline. "Blue-collar" workers are being replaced by automation, and more and more people work in the service industries, where unions are non-existent or weak. Today, less than 7 per cent of employees in the private sector are organised in unions.

Information Technology

Silicon Valley

The explosive growth of the Internet since the mid-1990s has generated a booming information technology (IT) services industry, with an area south of the **San Francisco Bay Area** as its main centre. The place was labelled "Sili-con Valley" because silicon is the base material of the semiconductors used in computer circuits. The computer-related history of the valley dates back as far as 1938, when students Bill Hewlett and David Packard started producing electronic equipment on the advice of Frederick E. Terman, then professor at **Stanford University** in Palo Alto. In the 1950s, Hewlett-Packard and others moved to the new industrial park of Stanford University, where in the course of the next few decades many other young and entrepreneurial people started their businesses. When in the mid-1980s chip manufacturing in Silicon Val-ley came to an end because of powerful Japanese competition the firms shift-ed their business field from hardware to software production. New jobs were created and the export rate boomed with the arrival of young start-ups and the settlement of other industries such as biotechnology and environmental science. Many of these start-ups have grown into big multinational compan-ies, such as Apple or Google (part of Alphabet Inc.).

Today a large number of IT companies employ engineers to develop and design entertainment software (e.g. video games) and electronic commerce applications. Skilled experts are needed to cope with the growing volume of online and offline transactions, web searches and social media interactions from billions of smartphones and mobile devices. Since many companies have begun to store their data "in the cloud" jobs have increased for people to work in cloud computing services and cloud security. As a result, America's IT sec-tor, including telecommunications, makes significant contributions to the US economy, and is the world's leading innovator in digitalisation.

Bill Gates and Steve Jobs

Americans don't like monopolies – and what happened more than one hundred years ago to Rockefeller's Standard Oil seems to have repeated itself in the US Department of Justice's action against software giant **Microsoft**. The company was founded by computer programmer William Henry Gates, who is one of the wealthiest people in America today. Bill Gates was born in Seattle in 1955 and wrote his first software programme when he was only 13. As a high school student he helped computerise the payroll system of his school. At the age of 15, he founded a company that constructed a device to control traffic patterns in Seattle which he sold to local governments. In 1975, when he was in his second year at Harvard, Gates joined his friend Paul G. Allen and began adapting Basic, a popular programming language used on large computers, for use on smaller **personal computers (PCs)**. Later in the same year, he dropped out of Harvard to devote his whole time writing programmes. In 1976, together with Allen, Bill Gates founded Microsoft to develop and produce a computer operating system called MS-DOS (Microsoft Disk Operating System). The rise of the company began in 1981 when the world's

Bill Gates (right) and Steve Jobs at a conference in California in 2007

biggest computer supplier **International Business Machines (IBM)** adopted Microsoft's software DOS for its line of personal computers. Gates was smart enough not to sell his software, but to license it to IBM, which means he received revenues for every computer sold. Makers of IBM compatible PCs also turned to Microsoft for their basic software, so that soon Gates had licensed DOS to more than 100 vendors, making it the dominant operating system. Before the age of 40, Gates had made tens of billions of dollars, which made him the world's richest private individual. He owns a collection of expensive sports cars and built himself a $50 million computer-controlled private complex overlooking Lake Washington. In 1995, he published his bestseller *The Road Ahead* where he observed, "Success is a lousy teacher. It seduces smart people into thinking they can't lose". As Microsoft's products began to dominate the market of computer operating programmes, many of Gates' rivals saw the influence and power of Microsoft with suspicion. In 2000, Gates gave up his position as chief executive officer (CEO) of Microsoft. In the same year, together with his wife Melinda, Bill Gates started the **Bill & Melinda Gates Foundation**. The couple use large sums of their fortune to improve healthcare and reduce poverty in developing countries. They put special emphasis on the fight against malaria and HIV. Gates and his wife also donate money to universities, educational institutions and libraries worldwide.

Steve Jobs was a technology pioneer and businessman who built one of the world's most successful and innovative IT companies from humble beginnings, thus exemplifying the American Dream. Jobs was born in 1955 and raised by his adoptive parents in the San Francisco Bay Area. After graduating from school, he briefly attended college in Portland, worked for Atari as a video game designer and travelled to India. Back in California he set up his own business together with his friends Steve Wozniak and Ron Wayne in his parents' garage. In 1976, they founded a company which they called **Apple**. As Jobs wanted to make computers work for everyone, he looked at them more as a user, not as an engineer. With this approach, he revolutionised the production of a series of user-friendly and beautifully designed electronic devices. In 1984, Jobs presented the legendary Macintosh, the first commercial computer which was mouse-driven and had a graphic user interface. However, the product did not sell well, and after an internal power struggle Jobs left Apple. In 1985, he founded NeXT, which manufactured computer workstations, and bought Pixar Animation Studios, which later produced hits like *Toy Story*. When Apple ran into trouble, also because Microsoft's Windows software had become the standard on computers worldwide, Jobs was called back in 1997 as chief executive, and Apple's rise as the most innovative IT company began. In January 2007, Steve Jobs presented a small electronic device made of plastic and metal with the words "This will change everything". His promise has come true. The **iPhone** opened up a new era of communication, sometimes referred to as "the smartphone age". Smart mobile phones are in fact small computers which offer Internet access everywhere and have since revolutionised how people communicate or get things done. The iPhone has been the big earner for Apple, making the company one of the world's most valuable IT firms. Other Apple products such as the iPod and the iPad did not exceed the iPhone's huge success as the fastest-selling gadget in history. Steve Jobs died in 2011, but his legacy as a grand visionary lives on.

Finance

The US financial centre is situated in **Wall Street** in lower Manhattan, where banks, insurance companies and investment firms have offices. The world's most important place for traders to sell and buy investments, to raise capital for business, the **New York Stock Exchange** (NYSE), is also located in Wall Street. A bell rings to mark the beginning and the end of each trading day. Every time an important company "goes public", which means that it sells shares to the public, the event is widely publicised. In 2012, for example, the founder and CEO of Facebook, Mark Zuckerberg, rang the opening bell when his company was listed on the stock exchange.

Two events (in 1929 and 2008) illustrate the dominance of Wall Street as a financial centre not only for the USA, but for the whole world. When Wall Street is in trouble, economic consequences can be felt all over the globe. At the end of the 1920s, the Dow Jones index fell, indicating the arrival of a recession, a slump in business. Investors panicked and sold their stocks in large quantities. Values fell dramatically and led to the crash of the New York Stock Exchange in October 1929. The crash marked the beginning of what became known as "The Great Depression". A severe economic decline hit the US and spread to Europe; mil-

The New York Stock Exchange (on the right) in Wall Street

lions lost their jobs and were thrown into abject poverty. In 2008, Wall Street nearly collapsed following the crisis on the housing market. However, Wall Street did not get into trouble because of economic and political upheavals, it was extremely well-paid employees of investment banks who created havoc by gambling with high risk financial instruments, which had become possible by deregulation in the finance sector. To prevent abusive practices in the financial industry and to protect the American taxpayer from bailouts for failing banks, the US administration introduced several **financial reforms**. In

2010, for example, President Obama signed the Dodd-Frank Wall Street Reform and Consumer Protection Act.

In 2011, Protestors against unbridled speculation and risky transactions founded the **Occupy Wall Street** movement. They took to the streets with the slogan "We are the 99%", which expressed that the wealth of the country was in the hands of a tiny minority and the overwhelming majority had to be satisfied with declining incomes or had next to nothing to live on. For many, Wall Street is the place where the country's wealth is generated, for others it is the symbol of ruthless capitalism.

Sports

Sport is an important part of American life. Going to a sporting event is a favourite pastime, and many Americans take their families for a day out to a stadium or a sports hall. Eating popcorn, hotdogs and ice-cream, drinking coke, watching the cheerleaders, enjoying the music of the brass band and, most important of all, cheering the home team makes for perfect entertainment. The sellers of food, drink and souvenirs at the stadiums do good business as well. Millions watch sports at home in front of their TV sets. The **Super Bowl game**, which is the championship final in US professional football, attracts the largest audience every year. Firms pay enormous sums to advertise during this broadcast. For other Americans sport is not only a source of entertainment, they practise it to keep fit. The number of runners and joggers has increased since the fitness craze swept the United States. In numerous health and fitness clubs people "work out", and hundreds of magazines, books and videos inform them how to do it properly and what equipment is needed. These examples illustrate the close connection between sport and business – sport is a big money-maker today. Every year the thriving sports industry in the United States earns billions of dollars and employs thousands of people in the services and manufacturing sectors.

The recent history of the Olympic Games shows the close connection and **interdependence of sport, television and industry**. At the Olympic games of Los Angeles in 1984, the Americans showed the world how to profit from the games through sponsorship. For the first time, multinational corporations (e.g. McDonald's) signed on as official sponsors who bought the rights to use the Olympic emblem on their products and place advertising posters around the arenas and tracks. The fact that the Games attract a large viewing audience makes the Olympics an ideal platform for advertising. Commercial television stations need large audiences to sell their time to advertisers and consequently pay out huge amounts of money to secure the rights to broadcast the event. America's National Broadcasting Company (NBC) paid $4.38 billion for exclusive US broadcast and cable TV rights to the four Olympic Games between 2014 and 2020. Most of the money which is earned in sport comes from television. Revenues from ticket sales alone cannot finance big sporting events. Such is the influence of the TV companies that sometimes the rules of the game or time tables are changed to allow for better TV coverage. In tennis, the "tiebreaker" was introduced to shorten televised matches, time-outs are used to show commercials, and most baseball matches take place at night, because this is the best time ("prime time") to reach a large audience. Several (industrial action) **strikes** which were staged in the past underline the fact that sport has turned into an industry. In the season 1994/95, for example, the Major League baseball players went on strike, and in 1999, the basketball players refused to play until their pay was raised. Organised labour and collective bargaining have become an integral part of professional sports. Professionals earn as much money as film stars and know very well that team owners, TV companies and advertisers depend on their performance. Critics may deplore the continuing commercialisation of sports but there is no turning back the clock.

In Europe, there are sports clubs which organize games and matches – in the US it is the high schools, **colleges and universities**. When a college or a university has outstanding players among its ranks it not only increases the prestige of the institution, it is also important for its financial situation. Colleges and universities have to find their own resources and good money can be earned with a first-class football or basketball team. As a result, many colleges have resorted to granting **scholarships** to athletes because of their skills as sportsmen and less because of their academic abilities. Critics ridicule this fact, saying that in the American system "scholarships are given to illiterate football players". The **close connection between professional and college sport** is also illustrated by the fact that many professional football and basketball teams pick promising younger players from high school or college teams. The selecting of young college players to include them into professional sides is called "drafting". The annual football draft is broadcast live on TV.

Apart from the economic side there are also **social and political aspects** connected with sport. Sometimes sport is used for political aims. At the 1968 Olympics in Mexico two black US medallists raised their fists, the Black Power salute, in protest against racial discrimination while the American national anthem was being played. During the Cold War both superpowers exploited the Olympics as a forum for political protest. In 1980, the United States led a boycott of the Olympic Games in Moscow because the Soviet Union had invaded Afghanistan. In retaliation, the Soviet Union and further 13 Communist countries withdrew their athletes from the 1984 Olympics in Los Angeles.

Sport has also helped to **climb in society**. Many poor boys and girls, often from black families, have achieved social recognition and economic success because of their athletic excellence, thus realising their American Dream in the world of sport.

American Sports Inventions

The sporting events, apart from the Olympic Games and soccer, which draw the largest crowds and with which TV stations achieve the highest ratings, are sports which were invented in the United States.

American Football

The Europeans have soccer – or association football – the Americans have a different sort of football which is a mixture of rugby and soccer. American football was first played in US colleges in the mid-19th century, and the first rules were drawn up at Princeton College in 1867. The game, which is played between September and January, resembles rugby, but forward passing of the ball is permitted. The object of the teams – 11 players are allowed on the field for each team at any one time – is to score touchdowns, which means to move the ball across the opposite goal line. One or more defensive players of the opposing squad attempt to bring the ball carrier down to the ground by tackling. Professional football is organised by the **National Football League**, which consists of two groups, called

For many Americans, football is the most exciting team sport. The Super Bowl game is a huge national event.

conferences, the American Football Conference (AFC) and National Football Conference (NFC). At the end of each season the winners of the two conferences meet in a series of play-off games each January for the **Super Bowl** (instituted in 1967) to determine the national champion. An outstanding American football player was Walter Payton of the Chicago Bears – or "Sweetness", as he came to be known – who gained more yards and scored more touchdowns than any other running back by the time he retired. Another hero of the game was Orenthal James Simpson, who came from San Francisco. He was nicknamed "The Juice", because of his initials O. J. which also stand for "orange juice", and he gained fame as one of the best and fastest running backs. After his football career Simpson worked as a sports commentator and appeared on television and in several films. In 1995, he was charged of killing his ex-wife and her friend. At the end of a sensational double murder trial which was televised worldwide Simpson was acquitted of the murder charges, but there are doubts about his being innocent. He never got back on track and in the meantime has been to prison for felonies such as armed robbery.

Baseball

Baseball is the national pastime in the USA. For Europeans, it is probably the most puzzling sport (similar to cricket or "rounders"), but it has become an integral part of the American way of life. It is said that even Abraham Lincoln played baseball and was so fascinated by it that he kept a delegation of politicians waiting who had come to inform him of his nomination for the presidency until he had finished batting. At the beginning of the century, a committee was set up to find out the origins of the sport and eventually came to the conclusion that Abner Doubleday, a West Point cadet, had invented baseball in 1839. However, these findings are doubtful, because there is evidence that the sport was played much earlier. Alexander Cartwright drew up the first rules in 1845. Baseball is played between April and October on a field which is laid out in the form of a square, called a diamond, by two sides of players with a bat and ball. Professional teams usually consist of 9 players each on the field. The aim of the game is to score as many runs as possible. A run is scored every time a player has made a complete circuit of the three bases and has returned to home plate. The visiting team goes up to bat first. The aim of the team in the field is to keep the batters from scoring by catching the ball. When a ball is hit out of the playing field, or if fielders cannot throw the runner out before he reaches home, the hit is good for four bases, or a homerun.

Baseball is a typically American sport which was invented in the first half of the 19th century.

The two major professional groups are the **American League** and the **National League** (15 teams each), with each league having East, Central and West divisions. In addition to the major leagues there are minor leagues in many American cities. The professional teams earn billions of dollars from ticket sales, the sales of food and drink, and television and marketing rights. Baseball players are regarded as the best paid professionals in the world of sport. At the end of a season the winners of the leagues determine in a best-of-seven games **World Series** the world champion. Famous teams include the

New York Yankees, most frequent winner of the World Series, the **Chicago White Sox** and the **Toronto Blue Jays**, a Canadian team which won the World Series in 1992 and 1993. Baseball is becoming increasingly popular in Japan and Latin America. To honour Abner Doubleday and the heroes of the game the National Baseball Hall of Fame was dedicated in 1939 in Coopers-town, N.Y., where Doubleday had laid out his baseball field 100 years before. One of the first five players elected to the Baseball Hall of Fame was George Herman "Babe" Ruth (1895–1948). Ruth was born into a very poor family in Baltimore and became one of the most popular figures of professional base-ball. He was the best left-handed pitcher in the American League and for a long time held a record of 60 homeruns in a season. Ruth played for the Bos-ton Red Sox, the New York Yankees, the Boston Braves and at the height of his career he was the highest paid player of his time. In 1935, he played his last season and later became coach of the Brooklyn Dodgers. One of the best fielders of the New York Yankees was Joe DiMaggio (1914–1999), nicknamed Joltin' Joe and the Yankee Clipper, who holds the record for hitting safely in 56 consecutive games. His second wife was the film star Marilyn Monroe.

Basketball

Basketball is a sport which is truly American in origin and has no European ancestors like American Football (a mixture of rugby and soccer) or baseball (England's cricket). Since its invention by James A. Naismith, a physical educa-tion instructor at the YMCA Training School in Springfield, Massachusetts, in 1891, it has always enjoyed great popularity. As a student Naismith played rugby, but he was put off by the rough side of it and thought about a new indoor ball game that would rule out physical contact. He chose elevated goals to minimize force on the ball and to keep some distance between the players and the actual scoring. As he could not find boxes to make the goals he used peach baskets. That is why the game became known as 'basketball' and not 'boxball', as the inventor had first intended to call it. The metal hoop was in-vented in 1906 and a bag of braided cord netting was attached to it. Today the game is practised all over the country on playgrounds and driveways. Al-though a few of the original principles of basketball have survived – offensive or defensive fouls are penalised to avoid physical contact – modern basketball has a wholly different look today. Five players make up a basketball team – a centre, two forwards, and two guards – and the aim of the game is to throw the ball through the opponent's basket, situated at the end of the court, and 10 ft (3.05 m) above the ground. Almost all professional basketball players are well over 6 ft (1.8 m) tall. The games are organized by the **National Basketball**

Association (NBA), which receives enormous sums from radio and TV stations for the rights to broadcast NBA games. The players also profit from the boom and basketball superstars earn millions of dollars. The NBA formed a panel of experts to select the 50 greatest players in its history, without regard to position. Among them are legends such as Kareem Abdul-Jabbar, the inventor of the skyhook ("Hakenwurf"), Magic Johnson, famous for his no-look pass, Michael "Air" Jordan, Hakeem Olajuwon and Shaquille O'Neal.

Kareem Abdul-Jabbar's original name was Lewis Ferdinand Alcindor, and he was born in New York City in 1947. In 1971, he adopted an Arabic name, which means "noble, powerful servant", when he converted from Catholicism to Islam. Scouts of the professional teams spotted him when he studied at the University of California. In 1969, he was selected by the Milwaukee Bucks in the NBA College Draft. In this annual draft, the best college players are chosen by the professional NBA teams. The basic idea of the draft system is to provide a chance for the weaker teams to improve themselves, therefore the team with the worst record in the league is allowed to draft first. In the meantime, the method has been changed. Since then the teams that do not qualify for the play-offs enter a luck-of-the-draw lottery, the winner of which has the first choice. Kareem was exceptionally tall (2.18 m) and he took advantage of his height to develop his signature shot, the "skyhook". He moved to the Los Angeles Lakers in 1984, and retired in 1989 with an exceptional list of achievements: No NBA player had ever scored more points, blocked more shots, won more Most Valuable Player Awards, played in more All-Star Games or performed at an older age.

Michael (Jeffrey) Jordan was born in Brooklyn in 1963. He played with the Chicago Bulls from 1984, leading the team to four world championships and was a member of the USA Olympic gold medal-winning team in 1984 and 1992, the "Dream team". Due to his remarkable fitness Jordan could jump higher than anybody else – a fact which earned him the nickname "Air Jordan". He left the game in 1999. Another basketball superstar was "Magic" Johnson, who shocked the sports world in 1991, when he announced his immediate retirement from professional basketball because he was HIV-positive. Earvin Johnson was born in Michigan in 1959. He was drafted in the Los Angeles Lakers in 1979 when he played for his hometown Michigan State University. Johnson became famous for his blind passes (no-look-passes).

American Sports Legends

Football, baseball and basketball are the most popular sports in the United States, but American athletes are in the world top class in many more disciplines as well. Americans love winners and sportsmen or sportswomen with singular merits are never forgotten. In **boxing**, Muhammad Ali enjoyed the reputation of a living legend – decades after winning his gold medal at the 1960 Olympic Games in Rome. Ali, who was born as Cassius Clay, won three world heavyweight championships and was renowned for his unique style of fighting which distinguished him from all other heavyweight boxers. "He floated like a butterfly and stung like a bee", fans praised Ali enthusiastically. Muhammad Ali also became an idol for millions of African Americans in their fight for Civil Rights. Ali suffered for years from Parkinson's disease and died in 2016, aged 74.

Portrait of boxing legend Muhammad Ali

In **swimming** America's sports legends include Johnny Weissmuller (1904–1984) and Mark Spitz. Weissmuller, whose parents immigrated to the United States from Austria, participated in the 1924 and 1928 Olympic Games and won five gold medals. After his sport career he became a movie actor and starred in several films as Tarzan. Mark Spitz (born 1950) won seven gold medals in all events in which he participated at the 1972 Olympics in Munich – two more than the previous record holder. Swimmer Michael Phelps became the most decorated athlete in the history of the Olympic Games, holding 28 Olympic medals, 23 of them gold medals.

Fans of **track and field** events will always remember Jesse Owens, Bob Beamon and Carl Lewis. Jesse Owens (1913–1980) won four gold medals in track and field events at the Olympic Games of 1936 in Berlin, staged by the Nazi regime as a demonstration of the alleged superiority of the "Aryan", or white, race. This aim was seriously undermined when the African American athlete James Cleveland (Jesse) Owens achieved his Olympic triumphs. Bob Beamon (born 1946) shot to fame with a single jump he took at the 1968 Summer Olympic Games in Mexico City. Aided by Mexico City's thin air, Beamon landed at 8.90 metres, setting up a record which stood until 1991. After the Olympic Games Beamon never jumped more than 8.20 metres because he was plagued by a hip injury and he retired before the 1972 Olympics. Carl Lewis (born 1961) – together with Al Oerter – is the only athlete to win four Olympic gold medals in the same track-and-field event. At the 1984 Summer Games in Los Angeles, he equalled Jesse Owens' feat of the 1936 Olympics in Berlin by winning gold medals in the long jump, 100 metres, 200 metres, and the 4×100 metre relay. When Lewis ended his Olympic career he had won nine gold and one silver medal altogether.

The list of outstanding athletes is almost endless. **Tennis** supporters admire Bill Tilden (1893–1953), the first American tennis player to win the men's singles at Wimbledon in 1920, or Billie Jean King, Martina Navratilova, John McEnroe, Pete Sampras, and Venus and Serena Williams. For **ice hockey** fans Canadian Wayne Gretzky is the greatest player of all time, who ranks with basketball's Michael Jordan and soccer's Pele as one of the greatest athletes of the 20th century. Gretzky played for the Canadian team Edmonton Oilers – members of the American **National Hockey League** (NHL) since the 1979 to 1980 season –, and later in Los Angeles, St. Louis and New York. He scored more goals in a season than anybody else and in 1993 became the highest-paid player. When he retired in 1999, the NHL decided never to use his jersey number (99) again.

Americans live in a competitive society, and the world of sport is a reflection of it. Doing sport just for the fun of it is becoming a rarity. At the centre of sports which receive nationwide media coverage is competition and the fight for financial profit. The spectacular rise and fall of two American sports heroes, Marion Jones and Lance Armstrong, illustrate the negative side of the commercialisation of modern sports. Track and field athlete Marion Jones, world champion and winner of five medals at the 2000 Olympics in Sydney, was tested positive to steroid use in 2006. In 2007, she admitted taking steroids before the Sydney games and lost all her medals. Racing cyclist Lance Armstrong owed his numerous victories, among them seven triumphs at the world's most important cycle race, the Tour de France, to continued use of **performance-enhancing drugs**. In 2012, he was stripped of all his titles and banned from professional cycling for life.

The USA – A World Power

Different Views of the United States

Hollywood, Mickey Mouse, McDonald's and Hemingway – ask people what comes to their mind when they think about America and you will get hundreds of different answers. To many, America is the **"land of promise, the land of the free"** – the dream land where the streets are paved with gold, the land of opportunities: "From dishwasher to millionaire". This is the impression people have who live in poverty, in authoritarian regimes, in countries of war and unrest, people who would like to get away from their homelands and make a fresh start. It is the America of illegal Mexican immigrants, and of refugees from war-afflicted zones in Africa and the Middle East, for example. The underprivileged and dispossessed of the world still hang on to this view of the United States.

To others, America is the "devil across the sea", the superpower which interferes in the inner affairs of countries around the world as soon as America's political or economic interests are endangered. It is the image of a nation which plays the policeman and acts in the name of liberty and democracy but which, in reality, pursues its own selfish interests. In some Asian and Middle East countries, the USA is regarded as a hostile imperial power and more than once, in times of crises, **anti-American feelings** erupt in violent attacks against US installations: Embassies are attacked or the American flag is burned. America is also seen as the country where violence and the use of guns has become widespread, where people are ruthlessly "hired and fired" from their jobs, where millions live in poverty and have no social security. This is how the French historian André Kaspi explains the frequently negative view: "With the United States as the only source of world hegemony, and with American industrial and cultural influence so strong, there's a natural desire by other nations to assert their independence."

When the newly elected president of the United States is sworn in at the inauguration ceremony he delivers a keynote speech in which he hardly ever misses defining America's role in world politics. Like most of his predecessors, Barack Obama, for example, declared that America was determined to defend the rule of law and the rights of man, principles which, in contrast, are not on the agenda of his successor Donald Trump, whose main aim is to put "America first".

America's Rise to World Power

From Isolationism to Interventionism

For most of the 19th century, the interests of the people of the United States were concentrated on their own affairs. All efforts were directed at the conquest of new territories, pushing the frontier further west. Above all, the fight between the North and the South in the **Civil War** (1861–1865) was of paramount importance for the future of the Union. When the Civil War came to an end, the era of Reconstruction began. The main concern was to rebuild the Union politically and to promote the economic development of the country. The North had made emancipation, the freeing of all slaves, a war aim, and after the defeat of the Southern states the problem of how to secure the rights of the freed slaves as equal citizens arose. The wrecked plantation economy in the South had to be revived without the slavery system. The former slaves, too, had to cope with their new situation. Many stayed in the South, wandering around aimlessly, until they eventually returned to the plantations to take up work as tenants. Others headed north into the industrial areas of the US. All in all, Americans were fully occupied with their home affairs and were therefore not very interested in what was going on in Europe. That is why they kept to a principle of foreign policy which President James Monroe (1758–1831) had developed in his seventh annual address to Congress on December 2, 1823. The **Monroe Doctrine** became one of the foundations of US policy in the 19th century. In it James Monroe, the fifth president of the United States, declared that the interests of the US lay in North and Latin America. He warned European nations against interfering in the affairs on the American continent. At the same time, the US would not meddle in the affairs of European countries and their colonies. The Monroe Doctrine became one of the foundations of US policy in the 19th century and can be regarded as the United States' first confident declaration of its importance in global affairs.

By the end of the 19th century the United States had finally recovered from the devastating effects of the Civil War. Industrialisation was in full swing. New inventions and technologies brought about unprecedented economic growth and prosperity. The building of the railway helped the opening up of the continent by providing a connection between East and West. New machinery made the American agriculture the most efficient in the world. After the settlement of the Far West new markets for American products were needed and the country began to reach out beyond its frontiers into Latin America and the Pacific: Feeling strong enough to claim status as world power, America gave up its "splendid isolation". America's new role in the world was expressed by Theodore Roosevelt, the 26th president of the United States (1901–1909). Roosevelt believed America should play a major role in world affairs and exert more influence. As president he mediated an end to the Russo-Japanese war – an achievement for which he was awarded the Nobel Peace Prize in 1906. Theodore Roosevelt's foreign policy centred on a belief that strong countries survive while weak ones perish. He saw in Germany the greatest threat to the USA and supported the expansion of the US navy into a modern fleet. Roosevelt extended the Monroe Doctrine by declaring that the US would prohibit any non-American intervention in Latin American affairs. He also affirmed the right of the US to intervene in any country in the Latin American area which showed political unrest. Thus the United States, for the first time, took on the role as **"police power"**. This policy became known as the **Roosevelt Doctrine**. An example of the new imperialist policy of the United States was the landing of American marines in Haiti (1915) to put an end to struggles between the blacks and the mulattoes and re-establish order on the island. The US occupied Haiti until 1934. The majority of Americans, however, still remained uninterested in foreign policy. This view changed when World War I broke out in Europe.

The United States hesitated to enter the war, and only after President Woodrow Wilson's War Message to Congress did the mood in the country eventually change. This change was brought about by German submarine warfare and the sinking of the British vessels Lusitania (1915) and Sussex (1916). Both sinkings caused the loss of more than a hundred American lives, and when the Germans, despite promises not to sink merchant vessels, continued with their unrestricted submarine warfare, the Americans felt that the time to act had come. In 1917, the United States decided to join the allies in their fight against Germany. However, after the end of World War I and the signing of the **Treaty of Versailles** in 1919, the US withdrew from Europe. Britain and France were disappointed that the Americans did not join the **League of Nations** but wanted to return to their policy of isolationism in foreign politics once more.

The US was also hesitant to enter **World War II**, and only after a direct attack on the country did the Roosevelt administration take up the fight. The United States had tried for some time to stay clear of the British and French fight against Germany's Nazi regime. However, President F. D. Roosevelt supported the war effort of the British and French in various forms, by supplying the Allies with war material, for example. It was the Japanese air attack on the American naval port of **Pearl Harbor** (Hawaii) on December 7, 1941, which catapulted the US into the war. The invasion of American, British and Canadian forces on **D-Day**, June 6, 1944, in Normandy was a crucial step to Allied victory. On May 7 and 8, 1945, Germany surrendered and on September 2 the war in the Pacific ended with the surrender of Japan. On August 6, the US had dropped an **atomic bomb** on the Japanese city of Hiroshima, and on August 9, 1945, on Nagasaki, killing at least 129,000 people.

Atomic bomb on Nagasaki, 9 August 1945

After World War II, the Americans acted differently in comparison to World War I, as they did not turn their backs on European and world politics again. On the contrary, from 1945 the United States assumed a strong leadership in world affairs. Western European politicians welcomed this change in the attitude of US foreign policy because they felt that support from the United States was needed in the re-construction of Europe and the emerging conflict with the Communist Eastern bloc. The US played the leading role in the creation of the **United Nations Organisation (UNO)** and of the **North Atlantic Treaty Organisation (NATO)**, the Western military defence alliance.

Policy of Containment

The US and its partners wanted to prevent the Soviet Union from extending its influence in Eastern and Central Europe by installing Communist governments. Therefore, the Americans adopted a new strategy towards the Soviet Union, which was called **Policy of Containment**. On March 12, 1947, President Harry S. Truman announced economic and military support for Greece and Turkey to prevent their falling under Soviet control. To oppose Communist expansion in Europe the United States lent a strong helping hand in the re-building of a devastated Europe **(European Recovery Program or Marshall Plan)** to avoid a political and economic vacuum in Central Europe, in particular. The **Truman Doctrine** contributed to the formation of two bitterly opposed blocks: the United States with its Western European allies on one side and the USSR and Communist bloc countries on the other. In contrast to a "hot" war, this struggle was carried out without direct warfare and was therefore termed **Cold War**.

In the 1950s, US senator Joseph R. McCarthy, a Republican from Wisconsin, created an atmosphere of **anti-communist hysteria**. By exploiting fears aroused by the Truman administration of a radical subversion of the American society McCarthy set out on a crusade to root out communism within the United States. A "Committee on Un-American Activities" investigated the lives and writings of many intellectuals and government officials. Most people who had to appear before the Committee could prove that they were innocent, but the lives of many were ruined.

During the Cold War the relationship between the Capitalist/Pro-American West and the Communist East was at freezing point. There were several serious confrontations, and there were fears that a third world war would erupt. Major confrontations were the building of the **Berlin Wall** (1961) and the **Cuban Missile Crisis** (1962), when the Soviets installed missiles on the doorstep of the USA, in Communist Cuba. To end the crisis, the Soviet Union withdrew its missiles from Cuba, and the US secretly agreed to withdraw its nuclear intermediate-range ballistic missiles from Italy and Turkey.

US Jupiter missile

The **arms race** and the **race in space** must also be seen in the light of the fierce competition between the two superpowers. Both wanted to prove to the world the superiority of their political and economic systems. In 1957, the USSR had put Sputnik, a small aluminium satellite, into orbit. This caused a shock in America, which was trailing behind in the development of rockets and satellites. The Soviet achievement was seen as a challenge and efforts were increased, which meant more money was made available to form a US space programme. In 1960, President **John F. Kennedy** committed the United States to landing a man on the Moon before 1970. As soon as the **Apollo Program** had succeeded, on July 20, 1969, in landing two astronauts on the moon, funds were reduced once again, because the free West had won the race in space.

Conflicts Abroad and at Home

America's Tarnished Image

In the first years after World War II the United States was seen as the liberator from Nazi Germany and the defender against Communism. However, gradually the image of the unselfish and unerring leader of the free West began to crumble and relations between the European allies and the United States cooled down. The Britons were the first to feel a certain amount of disappointment with their former war ally.

Many Britons were convinced that America used its power ruthlessly to bring about Britain's downfall as a leading world power by helping to dismantle the British Empire and replace it by American power. So Britain felt left alone by the US in the **Suez crisis**. In 1956, the Egyptian President Nasser had seized the Suez Canal, which was to a large extent owned by British and French stockholders. When forces of Britain, France and Israel tried to occupy the canal zone, the United States did not support its European allies, perhaps for fear of a Soviet counter attack. The majority of British politicians believed that the United States was doing everything possible to weaken Britain's political status in the world.

In other European countries like France and Germany, the American image was being tarnished by the reluctance of the Americans to grant equal rights to their black countrymen and by military and political interventions which resulted from America's Policy of Containment. This strategy often narrowed the views of the country's political leaders and made them take decisions which, seen from today, must be judged as foreign policy blunders. Some of these mistakes were made during John F. Kennedy's presidency: the beginning of American involvement in Vietnam and the **Bay of Pigs disaster**. Because of Kennedy's untimely, violent death (he was assassinated in Dallas on 22 November 1963) and the fact that the media turned him into a myth, his political errors were covered up for a long time. Only in recent years have historians started to paint a more realistic picture of Kennedy's political weaknesses. In April 1961, for example, he ordered approximately 1,500 Cuban exiles, organised and financed by the US Central Intelligence Agency (CIA), to land on **Cuba** at the Bay of Pigs. Their mission was to overthrow the revolutionary regime of Fidel Castro, who in 1959 had turned Cuba into a Communist country. The operation was a complete failure. The invaders were captured and in the following trial in Havana the United States was exposed to the world as the mastermind of the plan driven by imperialist striving for power. Even more disastrous was Kennedy's decision to send US soldiers to the Far East to fight Communism in war-torn Vietnam.

The **Vietnam War**, which lasted from the mid-1950s until 1975, was the second war in Vietnam. In the First Indochina War, Vietnamese nationalists had fought for independence from the French colonial regime. In the summer of 1954, France and Vietnam signed the Geneva Peace Accords, in which the temporary partition of Vietnam at the 17th line of latitude was laid down to allow France a face-saving defeat. It was also agreed that in 1956 Vietnam would hold national elections with which the temporary division of the nation would end. The United States, however, did not support the Geneva Accords because it was thought they granted too much power to the Communist Party of Vietnam. Consequently, when the regime in South Vietnam under Ngo Dinh Diem refused to hold the promised elections because they feared the popular nationalist Ho Chi Minh would win, the United States backed Diem's

refusal. The result was an escalating conflict between the Republic of Vietnam in the South, and the Communist Democratic Republic of Vietnam in the North led by Ho Chi Minh. The revolutionary movement of the Vietcong took up the fight against Diem's regime on southern territory. The US sent more and more combat troops to help Diem and started bombing military installations and cities in Northern Vietnam. The use of **chemical weapons** such as Napalm bombs and Agent Orange had catastrophic effects on people and the landscape. The backing of the Saigon regime and the cruelty of the bombings tarnished the image of

A US marine and an alleged Vietcong activist during a search and clear operation

the United States and roused massive protests in the USA and all over the world. On the streets of Saigon Buddhist monks killed themselves by setting fire to their bodies. The pictures of the monks engulfed in flames made world headlines. The Americans eventually had to admit their military power was ineffectual against the guerrilla tactics of the Vietcong. The Vietnam War, which President Kennedy and his successor President Johnson had meant to be "a limited war", ended with defeat. In 1975, a peace treaty was signed and Vietnam was formally reunified in 1976. The war, in the course of which the

US air force had dropped three times as many bombs as during World War II, had devastated Indochina and claimed the lives of about 58,000 Americans and as many as 2 million Indochinese. The war cost America over $150 billion, and it took the US economy several years to make up for the loss. However, the war in Indochina was not only a setback to the policy of containment in Asia, but more than anything else a shock to American self-confidence from which it has taken the nation much longer to recover. In films like *Apocalypse Now*, *Platoon* and *The Deer Hunter* the trauma of Vietnam is the central theme.

Unrest at Home and in Western Europe

It was not only the Vietnam War which raised doubts about America's self-complacency. At home there were problems, too, which cast a shadow on the world defender of human rights, personal liberty and democratic government. The 1960s were years of unrest when the Civil Rights Movement, the struggle of the African Americans for equal rights, gathered momentum. In this fight they gained world-wide support and the US government came under heavy fire abroad and at home. In the late 1960s, the protest against the Vietnam War and the arms race became stronger. In August 1968, clashes of antiwar demonstrators with the police and the National Guard occurred in Chicago around the Democratic Party's national convention. In Europe, too, young people in ever increasing numbers demanded the end of the Vietnam War, and the use of military force to achieve political aims. In 1979, the decision to deploy US Cruise and Pershing-II missiles in Britain and several other Western European countries led to protest marches or sit-ins, for example in the 1980s in Mutlangen, Germany, which was close to a US military base for Pershing II missiles.

Anti-war protests in Chicago (1968)

From the End of the Cold War to the 21st Century

The Policy of Détente and the End of the Cold War

By the 1970s, the United States began to pursue a policy of détente. The Soviet Union, being deep in economic difficulties, agreed to take up talks on **disarmament** to put an end to the costly arms race. Negotiations eventually led to two major agreements, SALT I and SALT II **(Strategic Arms Limitation Talks)** in 1972 and 1979 respectively, which provided for the limitation of defensive and offensive weapons. SALT II, however, was not ratified by the US because of the Soviet Union's invasion of Afghanistan in the same year. The United States increased its defence spending again during Reagan's presidency in the 1980s. Millions of dollars went into the **Strategic Defense Initiative (SDI)** programme, more commonly known as "Star Wars", a sort of military base in space. However, with the Soviet Union's new leader Mikhail Gorbachev, arms control talks were resumed in 1986, on a summit in Reykjavik, Iceland. In the late 1980s, the Communist bloc in Eastern and Central Europe began to disintegrate, and in 1990 the "Two Plus Four Agreement" between the Federal Republic of Germany, the German Democratic Republic and the four World War II allies (USA, France, Britain and the Soviet Union), paved the way for the re-unification of Germany. The Cold War had come to an end.

One of the factors which contributed to the **disintegration of the Soviet Union**, apart from a bleak economic situation, was the country's disastrous involvement in **Afghanistan**, when it intervened to support the communist government in its conflict with anticommunist Muslim insurgents, the mujahideen, which were backed by the United States. The US support of the Muslim rebels proved to have fatal repercussions as the very forces were nurtured that paved the way for Islamist terror, which hit the US on 9/11.

In 2014, a violent conflict in eastern Ukraine brought back memories and fears of the era of East-West confrontation. Ukrainian government forces and separatist rebels supported by Russian troops were engaged in heavy fighting. The USA and European countries imposed sanctions on Moscow in response to Russia's military advances on Ukraine and its annexation of the Crimea.

In the 1990s, after the disintegration of the Soviet Union and the collapse of the Communist bloc the United States held a stronger position in world politics than ever before. **President Bill Clinton** used America's new role as the only world leader to mediate in conflicts. He tried to conciliate between Palestinians and Israelis and he exerted his influence to promote a peace settlement between the conflicting parties in Northern Ireland. In several parts of the world US forces intervened. This time, however, under the auspices of the United Nations, in order to avoid the impression that America wanted to take advantage of its singular military and economic strength.

America's Role in the 21st Century

Profound changes came when America was attacked on **September 11, 2001** by Islamist terrorists. The death of 3,000 innocent people and the destruction of the twin towers of the World Trade Center, the symbols of Western capitalism, have had a fundamental impact on America and the world. The United States government set itself the target of not only defending the American territory but also of ridding the world of authoritarian regimes which, in the eyes of the US administration, represented a threat to security and world peace. For states like Iraq and other dictatorial regimes – the so-called "rogue states" ("Schurkenstaaten") – **President George W. Bush** coined the term

"axis of evil", an axis which by producing weapons of mass destruction posed a grave and growing danger to America and the free world. To combat these dangers, he proclaimed the **war on terror**, beginning in 2001 with the Americans invading Afghanistan. Bush counted on America's allies to join him in the effort. Supported by Britain's Prime Minister Tony Blair, he went on with his crusade with the invasion of Iraq in March 2003. With this decision Bush acted against the advice of the majority of the Security Council and several European nations (e.g. France, Germany) who expressed their wish to prolong the mission of the UN inspectors in Iraq whose job was to look for weapons of mass destruction – which eventually were never found. In-

The towers of the World Trade Center after being struck by the captured planes on September 11, 2001

stead the American government categorized countries into either good or evil ones – those who backed the American decision and those who didn't. Thus the debate over whether to go to war in Iraq provoked deep divisions between Europe and the US.

The election of **Barack Obama** in 2008 opened up a new era of US foreign policy. Whereas Republican presidents Bush (father and son) had kept to

Reagan's philosophy "peace through strength", which meant to use America's military power to guard its interests and influence worldwide, Democrat Obama redefined America's role in the world. Generally speaking, he aimed at addressing worldwide issues in a more cooperative way than his predecessors so that challenges such as the financial crisis, the protection of the climate and the fight against terrorist threats could be solved

US soldiers in Afghanistan

together. Although President Obama confirmed his conviction that the United States played an indispensable role in promoting international peace and prosperity, he started rebalancing America's foreign policy. He gave up the American role of policeman of the world and exercised **military restraint** – for example in the Middle East. In the devastating war in Syria, the US exercised air strikes, but only employed a limited number of ground troups to support the fight against ISIS and the Assad regime's army.

Obama's policy doctrine of **disengagement** was partly due to economic and social problems at home (economic crisis and enormous debt and deficit). By putting an end to extensive military commitments abroad more funds were made available to address issues in the US. As to the fight against terrorism Obama distanced himself from George W. Bush's military strategies in Iraq and Afghanistan, and promised to end both wars. Instead of employing more ground troops he stepped up the usage of unmanned aerial vehicles (drones), especially in Afghanistan, and promoted secret agent missions, one of which resulted in the killing of the founder of al-Qaeda, Osama bin Laden, in 2011. In the same year, Libyan dictator Gaddafi was killed following a military intervention of an international coalition in which the US played an important part. By the end of 2011, the American forces had left Iraq, but in 2014, troops returned to support Iraqi soldiers in their fight against ISIS.

Apart from the conflicts in the Middle East, the geopolitical situation in Asia is likely to play a more and more important role in the future. With **China** gaining enormously in economic and political power in the last few decades, the USA's focus has increasingly shifted to the **Asia Pacific region** where interests of the two powers may clash.

Stichwortverzeichnis

Bildnachweis

Titelbild: © ADDICTIVE STOCK-fotolia.de

S. 3, links: Engraving by Paul Revere, Boston, from a design by Henry Pelham 1770

S. 3, rechts: "The Destruction of Tea at Boston Harbor", lithograph 1846

S. 5, links: Portrait of George Washington, 1776 by Charles Willson Peale. Oil on canvas. Brooklyn Museum

S. 5, Mitte: Extracts from the votes and proceedings of the American Continental Congress held at Philadelphia, on the fifth of September, 1774. Philadelphia: Printed by William and Thomas Bradford, 1774

S. 5, rechts: Portrait of Thomas Jefferson, 1791 by Charles Willson Peale. Oil on canvas. Independence National Historical Park, Philadelphia

S. 8: U. S. Declaration of Independence, 1823 William Stone facsimile

S. 13: © Everett Historical. Shutterstock

S. 15: © Andrea Izzotti. Shutterstock

S. 18: © ullstein bild-Reuters

S. 21: US Capitol © Cristina CIOCHINA. Shutterstock

S. 22: © Ambient Ideas. Shutterstock

S. 25: US-Flagge © Rudy Balasko. Shutterstock

S. 28: Cecil Stoughton, White House Press Office

S. 30: Parteiembleme © Kamigami/Dreamstime.com

S. 42: Library of Congress, Prints and Photographs Division, ID LC-USZC4-1584

S. 43: Library of Congress, Prints and Photographs Division, ID LC-USZ62-12595

S. 46: National Archives, WPA Information Division, ID 518267

S. 47: Union Pacific Railroad

S. 49: Erlend Bjørtvedt, licensed under cc-by-sa-3.0

S. 52: Office of Representative Phil Gingrey 2007

S. 53: © Americanspirit/Dreamstime.com

S. 56: Library of Congress, Rare Book and Special Collections Division, ID LC-USZ62-44000

S. 58: National Archives, U. S. Information Agency, Record Group 306

S. 59: National Archives, U. S. Information Agency, ID 306-SSM-4A-35-6

S. 61: Library of Congress, Prints and Photographs Division, ID LC-USZ6-1847

Ihre Anregungen sind uns wichtig!

Liebe Kundin, lieber Kunde,

der STARK Verlag hat das Ziel, Sie effektiv beim Lernen zu unterstützen. In welchem Maße uns dies gelingt, wissen Sie am besten. Deshalb bitten wir Sie, uns Ihre Meinung zu den STARK-Produkten in dieser Umfrage mitzuteilen.

Unter *www.stark-verlag.de/ihremeinung* finden Sie ein Online-Formular. Einfach ausfüllen und Ihre Verbesserungsvorschläge an uns abschicken. Wir freuen uns auf Ihre Anregungen.

www.stark-verlag.de/ihremeinung

Richtig lernen, bessere Noten

7 Tipps wie's geht

1. **15 Minuten geistige Aufwärmzeit** Lernforscher haben beobachtet: Das Gehirn braucht ca. eine Viertelstunde, bis es voll leistungsfähig ist. Beginne daher mit den leichteren Aufgaben bzw. denen, die mehr Spaß machen.

2. **Ähnliches voneinander trennen** Ähnliche Lerninhalte, wie zum Beispiel Vokabeln, sollte man mit genügend zeitlichem Abstand zueinander lernen. Das Gehirn kann Informationen sonst nicht mehr klar trennen und verwechselt sie. Wissenschaftler nennen diese Erscheinung „Ähnlichkeitshemmung".

3. **Vorübergehend nicht erreichbar** Größter potenzieller Störfaktor beim Lernen: das Smartphone. Es blinkt, vibriert, klingelt – sprich: es braucht Aufmerksamkeit. Wer sich nicht in Versuchung führen lassen möchte, schaltet das Handy beim Lernen einfach aus.

4. **Angenehmes mit Nützlichem verbinden** Wer englische bzw. amerikanische Serien oder Filme im Original-Ton anschaut, trainiert sein Hörverstehen und erweitert gleichzeitig seinen Wortschatz. Zusatztipp: Englische Untertitel helfen beim Verstehen.

5. **In kleinen Portionen lernen** Die Konzentrationsfähigkeit des Gehirns ist begrenzt. Kürzere Lerneinheiten von max. 30 Minuten sind ideal. Nach jeder Portion ist eine kleine Verdauungspause sinnvoll.

6. **Fortschritte sichtbar machen** Ein Lernplan mit mehreren Etappenzielen hilft dabei, Fortschritte und Erfolge auch optisch sichtbar zu machen. Kleine Belohnungen beim Erreichen eines Ziels motivieren zusätzlich.

7. **Lernen ist Typsache** Die einen lernen eher durch Zuhören, die anderen visuell, motorisch oder kommunikativ. Wer seinen Lerntyp kennt, kann das Lernen daran anpassen und erzielt so bessere Ergebnisse.

Auf dem Smartphone
Interpretationshilfen

Buch inkl. eBook: Für den Durchblick bei komplexen literarischen Texten. Mit dem eBook den Lektüreschlüssel immer dabei haben.

▸ 🅔 Inkl. eBook, für alle Endgeräte, mit Online-Glossar zu literarischen Fachbegriffen

▸ Informationen zu Biografie und Werk, ausführliche Inhaltsangabe, gründliche Analyse und Interpretation

▸ Detaillierte Interpretation wichtiger Schlüsselstellen

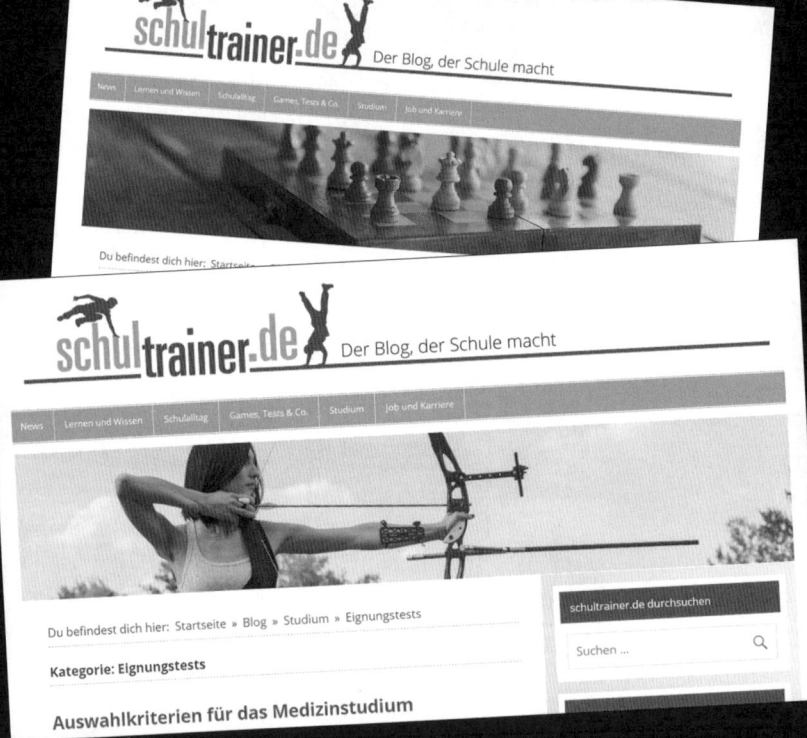